Seeking Christ in the
Crosses & Joys
of
Aging

by Ronda Chervin

Seeking Christ in the Crosses & Joys of Aging
By Ronda Chervin

ISBN #1-891280-31-7
Library of Congress Card #00-105307

Publisher:
CMJ Marian Publishers
Post Office Box 661
Oak Lawn, Illinois 60454
www.cmjbooks.com
jwby@aol.com

Manufactured in the United States of America.

Photo on cover: Robert E. Brandin and Granddaughter Rachel Anne with
permission.

Graphics for book: The Ridgefield Group

The publisher is grateful for permission to excerpt passages from these works:
Aging Successfully by George Lawton (Columbia University Press)
Angela of Foligno, The Complete Works, trans. by Paul LaChance,
O.F.M. (Paulist Press)
"Growing Old Gracefully" by Richard Johnson, Ph.D., Liguorian
Magazine, 1992

Contents

INTRODUCTION

<u>Seeking Christ in the Crosses and Joys of Aging</u> comes out of my struggle with what I now call the sixty's crisis. Unlike most people I know, I looked forward to becoming an old person, that is, until I arrived at my sixtieth birthday.

The biggest reason I had as a younger person for wanting to be old was admiration for sixty-plus mentors. When I became sixty, would I have some of their virtues: wisdom, serenity, exquisite beauty of soul and heart? I will tell you more about the lives of these holy men and women as we go along. For now, I want only to observe that many Catholics ardent in middle-age seem to take a quantum leap toward holiness around the age of sixty. And if they live on into their eighties or nineties their hearts become as soft as melted butter, with dispositions sweet, yearning and full of hope.

Thinking that devoutly Catholic Ronda might also advance in holiness at sixty, I imagined that I would feel happier and happier with each birthday of my late fifties. Quite the contrary. Losing a son to suicide at the age of fifty-four was the most piercing sorrow of my life. Losing my husband two years afterward compiled the misery. The pain of the deaths of my son and husband completely altered my previous idea of what nearing sixty would feel like. Instead of "mellowing out," I became a whirling dervish trying to find a new identity.

There were positives. It has been a gift from God to be able to be a live-in grandmother in the home of one of my married daughters in Arizona and to rejoice in another daughter's family in California. It was a beautiful and unexpected grace to be called to the consecrated religious life in a community that accepts women who want or need to dwell in their own homes. (See the conclusion at the end of the book for more information about this community).

Nevertheless, by the time of my sixtieth birthday, in 1997, I felt discouraged, old, and ugly. The usual aches, pains and fatigue that come with aging added to my unhappiness.

It was in this negative state of mind that I decided to start researching whatever came to hand from psychology and spirituality that might help me get through aging more gracefully. I planned a leisurely perusal of books and articles on my own shelves as well as an exhaustive examination of the wisdom of the saints. The project might span five years. I hired an excellent assistant, Judy Beshaw, to help. I am grateful for her skill in making selections from many helpful books. Elizabeth Valerius also added interesting items from research into heroes and heroines of aging.

After a year's work on the book, a pattern emerged. Key insights in secular writings came up again and again. As could be expected, the most important difference between the wisdom of the saints and the ideas of psychologists had to do with attitudes toward death. With one foot already in eternity, the saints experience the same crosses everyone else does in the aging process, but with a halo of hope around them. Life is short; eternity is infinitely long. Pain is hard, but hope of everlasting bliss in union with an already known and beloved Savior makes it bearable.

Noticing the same themes recurring in my reading, I decided on a shorter book with a more informal style. Instead of an exhaustive study, why not just let the reader accompany me in reacting to the ideas and inspiration I found along the way? During that first year I conducted a few workshops based on preliminary research. It was delightful to cull fresh insight from the participants. This led to the thought that some readers might want to register their own ideas about aging in their journals. Others might want to share insights in groups.

Questions for these purposes will be included at the end of each chapter.

The journey in search of the Christ who meets us in the crosses and joys of aging has been meaningful beyond initial expectations. Images and phrases from personal friends, literature, professionals, scripture, my own prayer and the lives of the saints now infuse themselves into my daily consciousness bringing laughter, understanding and hope.

As I begin sorting out my notes into book form, I pray: Dear God, you must know how difficult aging is for your human creatures. We believe that you sent your Son to redeem all the stages of life's way. Show us how to seek and find you in the crosses and joys of the last chapters of our lives.

FOR PERSONAL REFLECTION AND GROUP SHARING:

1. What have been your feelings about aging from childhood to the present?

2. Describe the lifestyles of people you have known well who aged well or badly in your own estimation.

3. How does your love of Christ and his for you enter into feelings about aging?

WHAT DOES AGING FEEL LIKE?

"Do not cast me off in the time of old age;
forsake me not when my strength is spent." (Psalm 71:9)
"They still bring forth fruit in old age,
they are ever full of sap and green." (Psalm 92:14)

General Perspectives

"There no child shall ever die an infant,

No old man fail to live out his life;

Every boy shall live his hundred years before he dies,

Whoever falls short of a hundred shall be despised...

My people shall live the long life of a tree."

(Isaiah 65:20-22)

Sixty years ago, when I was a child, living to the age of
one hundred was considered a horrible fate. Science-fiction
movies depicted the centenarian as a ghastly skeletal freak.
Nowadays, many sixty-year-olds have relatives in their
eighties and nineties! And sometimes these old people are
still strong, mentally alert, and even happier than the young
folk. As one friend of mine who teaches geriatrics pointed
out: aging is not a disease and not everyone declines! I am
told that a doctor in Switzerland interviewed all the people
in his country over one-hundred years old and found that
none of them led a sheltered life.

1

In light of this change in societal expectations, when I started my research for this book, I wanted to know more about what other older adults thought about both the joys and crosses of aging. Most likely we would be meeting Christ in the joys through gratitude and in the crosses by uniting our pain with his.

Asking friends and participants in workshops about positives and negatives of aging as they experienced them, I was surprised to see about an equal number of entries in the two columns! Of course, these random listings were not weighted. Chronic pain is only one item on someone's list, but clearly permeates daily life more than, say, the plus of senior discounts. Still, the long list of joys was heartening.

Perhaps you already think this book is going to be depressing. If so, consider the results of a survey about happiness. According to the account I read, the unhappiest people in the world are young white men, but the happiest are old black women! I bet you can guess why, too.

Here are the composite lists of pros and cons of aging I collected. Probably there are some omissions so obvious you can't believe it. They may appear in other chapters. If not, let me know for the second edition.

Positives

More Free Time, Less Pressure, More Security:
"I consider it a privilege to retire."
"I am less like a motorboat and more like a sailboat."
"Don't have to chauffeur kids around."
"I cherish solitude."
"It's nice to have more quiet in my life."
"Deciding myself what I will do most days feels so freeing."
"I find playing games, being silly with friends or siblings or pets even more fun than when I was a child."
"Time for travel."
"Hobbies like fishing, swimming, knitting, no longer have to

be squeezed in or justified, I can just relax with them."
"Freedom from sexual tensions can be a boon."
"Joy of social security, medicare, senior discounts."
"More able to say 'No!'"
"No P.T.A. meetings."
"Time to do less pressured volunteer work."
"I'm moving to a stage now where I have to retire from my retirement jobs."
"I do a lot still but it isn't work dependent on other people's approval; it's more relaxed when everything is up to me."

Glad Not to Be So Indispensable or Managerial:

"When it rains, I let it."
"Present accomplishments are not so important — the outcome seems more like God's doing and less my doing."
"I like being a background figure a lot more than in the past."
"It is pleasant to think of myself as drifting off into the horizon."
"Living vicariously through my adult children is less stressful."
"As a grandparent I can love children without being so responsible."
"Mellowed-out. Maybe because too tired to fight with people."
"Humble feeling that previous accomplishments are not so important."
"Enjoy being with my adult children."
"Don't have to go out when it snows."

Good not to have to Look Good:

"I used to worry a lot about how I looked. Now I don't care."
"Free to be me."

Living in the Past can be Enjoyable:

"Savoring happy memories is delightful."
"It makes me happy to recreate the past by living in ways my parents did."
"I've lived this long, and seen lots of things."
"It's healing to recall the fun of childhood."

I am Wiser:

"We've put a lot of time on life. We ought to be doing it well."

"It feels good not to go around full of illusions and ridiculous fantasies."

"There is so much rich and diverse experience to ponder."

"I have so much more knowledge than young people do."

"It is easy to be less worldly and more spiritual when you are older."

"Because I have more time to think, I have more perspective."

"I used to be full of self-doubt and irritation with myself. Now I have greater self-acceptance."

"My priorities are more realistic."

"Aging is discovering new truth, not always that can be expressed in words."

"More enjoyment of diversity."

I am Closer to God — Holier:

"Less concerned with ambitions, I am more benevolent."

"More time to contemplate and praise God for creation, like the way a dog wags his tail."

"Because of aches and pains, so grateful to God for everything pleasant."

"Can give lots away."

"I am more open to and feel the presence of God more."

"I can go to daily Mass and other services. These make me more loving."

"I came back to the Church after many years absence. It felt good to get rid of my sins in confession."

"I think a lot about eternal happiness, seeing my beloved dead again."

"Belief that I will live one day in a resurrected body is a consolation for the defects of my aging body."

Negatives

(As you read this list, you may feel discouraged. An antidote might be to put an "x" next to the ones that don't fit your reality or attitude toward this time of life. Another way to avoid being overwhelmed by the list might be to write in the margins as you read ways you have found to come against these feelings.)

Ugliness:

"Looking in the mirror, I see jowls, wrinkles."

"I long for my youthful face and figure."

"Sometimes I have the same facial expressions my mother and father had in old age; expressions I hated when I was younger."

"Young people and middle-aged people no longer look at me with interest because I am old, out of the loop. Like I don't even exist."

"You put on weight much faster on the same diet."

"It feels like I have no dignity as an elderly person. Just someone to ignore or cast out of sight."

Weakness:

"I hate lacking the flexibility, strength, and stamina of youth."

"I have less energy and speed in all activities."

"Don't feel useful."

"I put on weight too quickly."

"Small pressures rattle me."

"I feel stupid forgetting so much so often."

"I can't learn how to operate all the new technology."

"Having to do housework when I feel uncomfortable."

"Can't drive to church."

"Since turning sixty I have become much more indecisive about small and large matters. I feel like an idiot changing my mind ten times a day.

"I used to dislike having the day all scheduled up, 9-5, etc. But now I have too much freedom it seems."

"Old age used to be a privilege, now it is a condition."

Poverty or Relative Diminishment of Finances:

"I can't get work I could do because of agism."

"My pension and social security are not enough to live as I am used to."

"I have to choose sometimes between food and heating."
"I don't think I will ever pay off all my debts."
"Adult children need my money too much."

Fears:

"I am afraid of being a burden to relatives."
"The expression 'failing health' is so depressing."
"I am afraid of debilitating illness, especially terrible ones
like Alzheimer's"
"If I am too weak; they might put me in an old age home with
senile people. Or I might become totally senile."
"Fear of death and dying makes it impossible for me to sleep."
"I know my kids want my money. Maybe they will get rid of
me by euthanasia when I am too out of it to protest."
"Inertia is my problem. I have no get up and go."

Sadness:

"I feel unneeded and unwanted."
"It pains to have to give up favorite activities because I am
too ill or old, such as golfing or driving."
"Living with older children can be lonely if they are rarely home."
"It is like being a fifth-wheel to live with older children."
"I feel so lonely since my spouse died."
"I want to be in a committed relationship like my previous
marriage, not just among acquaintances."
"It is so terrible that my child died before me."
"My children rarely visit or call."
"It is so depressing to live alone or in a retirement or conva-
lescent home."
"Not enough respect in society — no manners in the young."
"Ridicule or even battering by adult children."
"I feel so low that only alcohol helps."
"No outlet for my knowledge and advice."
"I want to be more busy. All my life is not a vacation, and I
can't enjoy going on a vacation since everything is vacation."
"I would like to be close to my family but they don't want to
forgive and forget."
"People discriminate against me because I am old."

"Feeling of not having done enough with ones life."
"I suffer more now when I have to see how much sin and
suffering there is in the world. It is harder to accept now
than before.

Burdens:

"I am too old to have to take care of my more elderly relatives."
"Taking care of my grandchildren is too much for me."
"I am a burden to myself, so isolated and in a rut."
"I get cranky."
"I feel guilty for not having been a better person. But it's too
late."
"All the accumulated baggage of the pain in the hearts of
those I love is a burden to me."

Marital Problems:

"I want to sit home but my spouse wants to run around town
all day and wants me to go with her."
"Since we retired my spouse and I get on each other's nerves
like you wouldn't believe."
"My husband left me for a younger woman."
"It's annoying how in retirement we have different rhythms
for eating. When I want to eat my spouse has just finished
a large snack. We hardly ever feel hungry at the same time."
"My spouse is too depressed to have sex with me or even talk
to me. He or she refuses to go to counseling."

Physical Pain:

"I have so much pain I can hardly endure life."
"Pain keeps me from many former activities I loved."
"The different ailments I have cannot be alleviated because the
medicines that would help have too many bad side effects."
In other sections of this chapter, we will be going into
more detail about what aging feels like. Upcoming topics
include: dealing with the last part of life in *your own way*,
new sources of joy, loneliness and closeness, physical pain,
the approach of death, and heroes and heroines of aging.

8 Aging

Let us close this segment with a prayer:

Dear Lord Jesus, as I look through the list of positives of aging, I feel grateful for the ones I have experienced already. Thank you God for these gifts. I feel contrite about good parts of aging I take for granted and for which I never thank you. I thank you now. I wish for those pluses that are not yet part of my life. Please give them to me, if that be your will. As I look at the list of negatives, I feel thankful for not having had to go through all of them. I pray for others struggling with so many burdens. Please help them. Let me unite the pains of aging I know only too well to your sufferings, dear Jesus. Help me to bear them without despair. Give me hope in your promise of ultimate happiness for those who choose your way, and unexpected help from you even now on earth. Please add my tears to the pool of sorrows you transform into grace.

FOR PERSONAL REFLECTION AND GROUP SHARING:
1. Looking through the lists of positives and negatives. Which ones do you identify with? Check them. Compare your accounting with those of others you know.
2. Thank God for positives you have in your life and ask Him for strength and insight to deal with the negatives.

Doing It Your Own Way

"Bless the Lord who satisfies you with good as long as you live, so that your youth is renewed like the eagle's." (Psalm 103:5)

An intriguing theme came up over and over in my research. It was the resistance many elderly people put up to being forced into somebody else's ideas of what their aging should be like. "Doing it my way," is apparently not just a slogan for two-year-olds, teens, and young adults, but also for older adults. Since freedom is so much a part of the human person, why wouldn't aging people want to have choices about matters so personal as where to live, how to live, and even how many helpful relatives and friends they have offering advice at any given time!

In my own experience of aging so far I can see how doing it my own way comes in. Sure, I'm eager to listen to advice, but there are some areas, such as choice of friends, where I don't want any interference. I reason that even if I lose out sometimes because of unwise choices, still I'm willing to take that risk. To my anxious well-wishers, I want to say, "Hey, this is my life and you all just gotta put up with it."

In a later chapter the focus will be on how outspokenly Christian folk think about aging, but here I wish to present narratives about doing it your own way taken from the thoughts of many different kinds of people. I hope you'll enjoy these short tales as much as I did.

"The Year Alice Moved to the Attic," by Kathryn Etters Lovatt[1], describes the visit of an adult son to his old mother. He expects to find her in the living room of the old house, but to his surprise has to look around until he finally locates her in the attic! Alice has decided to spend most of her time in this upper story. She has made herself cozy living with old furniture and family antiques.

The son is worried. How can he be sure his mother is taking her medicines? But Alice doesn't care about pills. She doesn't think the soundness of her sleep matters much. She explains to her son that she began going to the attic just to look through things. Then, once, she got tired and fell asleep on a cot.

Alice's adult son will not accept the idea that his old mother, Alice, is not afraid to stay alone. The family worries because she doesn't answer the phone sometimes for weeks. They don't realize she can't hear the phone. The son wants to put her in a nice institution so he can feel she is safe.

Alice realizes finally that her son simply cannot understand her. She will just have to insist on aging her own way.
Alice reflects: "Little matter who came and went or sat or
stayed the night, she was alone. No one knew her anymore."[2]

Most of us would not go as far as Alice to insure isolation. We can be startled to find some of our friends moving
further in that direction than we would have yet decided to
go. Many seventy-year-olds of my acquaintance don't race
anymore to answer the phone the way I do. Instead, they let
the answering machine take calls hour after hour. Some
throw out most of the mail. I noticed that a friend who wrote
5 page, xerox letters, replete with joyful photos, for the last
twenty years, suddenly decided to send nothing! And sometimes I startle my friends by a new move toward greater
solitude. "What, you left for four days and didn't leave a
voice message to let us know!"

One of the books from which I will be taking the most
excerpts is called *The View in Winter: Reflections on Old
Age*.[3] It is written by a British sociologist, Ronald Blythe,
who interviewed hundreds of older people in the 1960's on
a variety of subjects. Here is a description of a gentleman as
eager to do things his own way as was Alice in the attic:

"At the time of the interview this man was an eighty-one
year old WWI veteran who had seen service in France. After
the war, he became a railwayman. He loved to return from
the British Isles to France on free passes. He had the easy
manners of the loner who was accustomed to making good
conversation with strangers in cafes, pubs and trains. Because he seemed scarcely to have so far been touched by the
usual deterioration of aging, he was not reconciled to being
an old man. Still living on his own, used to easy, detached
relationships, and quite unused to having anything done for
him, he was beginning to wonder, "What next?" While post-
First World War rites which meant so much to him — the

old comrades, associations, Armistice Day — had faded out, Frederick himself did not feel that *he* had faded. Inside, he was the dashing young Londoner in Rouen; outside, there was pressing advice about getting into an old people's home. It was for his own good, they would say. Anyway, he should think about it. *Think* about it? How unnatural for him to think like that! How odd that others should do so. It was not as though he has been a bother or ever asked a soul to do anything for him."[4]

Frederick and Alice are alike in wanting to do aging their own way. They do not want to be shunted off to an old-age home; at least not until they are totally disabled.

Maybe *your* way is like theirs. *My* way, I have always been very future oriented, is to think about old age homes now at sixty-one, in detail! Part of me is longing for the presumed comfort and security I might find there, even though I would be loathe to leave the delicious sounds and sights of the adults and grandchildren of my family.

The next excerpt, about dressing casually after retirement, fits me to a tee even though the clothing I am wearing is not sporty but a sister's outfit of loose blue dresses or jumpers with simple shirts underneath. Still, like Sarah Allen, I refuse to wear tight or uncomfortable clothing or shoes.

In the piece called, "Clay," Allen describes changes in her wardrobe after sixty:

"This year I bought six shirts, loose cotton...These and four pairs of shorts are my summer uniform. I no longer work in the outside world, struggling into clothes that conform to standards of current style and beauty. This freedom is a gift that pleases me anew each day. My body has stored a layer of plumpness around the middle where there was once a very small waist. I'm glad I enjoyed it while I had it. Sometimes I feel like I'm eternally four months pregnant, the stage when you become straight between chest and hips.

I've spent the last ten years of my life searching for dresses that swing from the shoulders, allowing movement and a sense of freedom...Dressing in the quiet apartment, I feel familiar dichotomy. The sudden panic of not having a schedule wars with the delight of a day to structure as I wish....I learn to move slowly, taking more time for small chores... There is an immense feeling of richness in my life...the busyness has been reduced to an essential lump of clay, wedged and cut on the wire of sixty-one years until all the air pockets are gone. There is a dense, heaviness that, devoid of extraneous material, is only myself. I can spin it through the coming days into a form that pleases me, pulling it up into a cylinder where the clay is thin and slippery, pressing it down again, pulling it out into a wide bowl to hold all that is me."[5]

Being free to age one's own way can also involve letting go of social expectations that would have seemed absolutes at a younger age. It would be clearly imprudent for a middle-aged person in business to offend potential customers, but proverbial is the old person who says whatever he or she pleases no matter how outrageous. Always a bit eccentric myself, I find that I am even more unwilling to conform as I have less to lose in terms of status or income.

Mrs. Dalloway, by Virginia Woolf[6], is a novel largely about aging. One of the issues in her story is men feeling like failures if they have not reached a certain level of wealth. Describing an old but still vital man who would have been expected to be more successful in the world than he turned out to be, Woolf writes:

"He was not old, or set, or dried in the least. As for caring what they said of him (the rich people), he cared not a straw — not a straw..."[7]

"The old have other things: compassion, comprehension, absolution."[8]

Non-conformity is one way of aging in an individualistic mode. So, perhaps, is eccentricity. A novel, *The Old Wives'*

Tale, by Arnold Bennett[9], describing long lives with unexpected old age scenarios, begins with this reflection in the introduction about freakish difference:

"An old woman came into the restaurant to dine. She was fat, shapeless, ugly, and grotesque. She had a ridiculous voice, and ridiculous gestures. It was easy to see that she lived alone, and that in the long lapse of years she had developed the kind of peculiarity which induces guffaws among the thoughtless. She was burdened with a lot of small parcels, which she kept dropping. She chose one seat; and then, not liking it, chose another; and then another. In a few moments she had the whole restaurant laughing...I reflected, concerning the grotesque diner: This woman was once young, slim, perhaps beautiful; certainly free from these ridiculous mannerisms. Very probably she is unconscious of her singularities. Her case is a tragedy...Every stout aging woman is not grotesque — far from it! — but there is an extreme pathos in the mere fact that every stout aging woman was once a young girl with the unique charm of youth in her form and movements and in her mind. And the fact that the change from the young girl to the stout aging woman is made up of an infinite number of infinitesimal changes, each unperceived by her, only intensifies the pathos..."[10]

The implication is that should someone have drawn the woman's attention to her eccentricities, she would no doubt have tried to justify them. Perhaps this passage could make us more compassionate to homeless old people on the streets.

Aging Successfully, by the psychologist George Lawton[11], is a book I will be quoting from in detail in a latter section of this book. Here I want to excerpt a manifesto that fits in well with the theme of aging your own way:

from *A Bill of Rights for Old Age*

The right to be treated as a person, as an individual, with the golden rule.

The right to be treated as an adult, not pushed around like
    children, or be patronized (being called girlie, etc.)
The right to make your own decisions, even if you will make
    mistakes.
The right to a future, don't say he's too old to change.
The right to have fun and companions.
The right to be romantic.
The right to be old and still around.
The right to work as long as possible.[12]
When I read passages such as the one from Lawton's
book, I stand straight, and stick out my chin defiantly, but it
is poems like the next one that warm my heart and offer
hope that someday I will be happy to be old:

I am becoming the woman I've wanted,
grey at the temples,
soft body...
Cracked up by life
with a laugh that's known bitter
but, past it, got better,
knows she's a survivor —
that whatever comes,
she can outlast it.
I am becoming a deep
weathered basket.

                  by Jayne Relaford Brown[13]

I was delighted to see a greeting card showing two
women in their 70's zooming on a motorcycle. They were
laughing excitedly, oblivious of the fact that they were being followed by a police car with his lights flashing! I feel
something like that whenever I do something unexpected,
different, "out-of-character." Last summer I had a chance to
try going on a jetski behind one of my sons-in-law. Even
though it was only for twenty minutes, the speed and the
waves jolted me completely out of my "blah-I'm-too-old-
to-live" feelings of just an hour before.

As I consider the question of doing it my own way, I pray:

My God, you created me to be just like everyone else but also different from everyone else. Let me not stagnate in my later years from over-conformity to dull images of aging. Let me not, either, be foolish, reckless, or inconsiderately eccentric. I long to be vital in spirit even if creaky in body. Help me be who you would like me to be.

FOR PERSONAL REFLECTION AND GROUP SHARING:
1. Reread passages in "Doing it Your Own Way" checking those that fit your own mentality, with an "x" next to those narratives that aren't "you" at all. Perhaps put a question mark next to any excerpts that bear thinking about more.
2. Talk about your reactions with relatives or friends.

New Sources of Joy

*"If you have gathered nothing in your youth,
how can you find anything in your old age?"* (Sirach 25:3-4)

One of the greatest sources of joy in aging is remembering. Unfortunately, it is connected up with one of the worst features: forgetting! It seems as if the more we regret not being able to remember things that happened 5 minutes ago, the more "space" we have in the memory-bank for things that happened years ago, many of them pleasant to recall. Sometimes we are also very happy *not* to be able to recall strongly unpleasant memories of the past.

We all know how embarrassing and inconvenient and sometimes even humiliating it is to forget things that are important for an efficient, smooth daily life. But here is a poem that is an invigorating witness to how forgetting can lead to new life. I think you will find it thought-provoking even if you don't agree with the writer's politics.

After Sixty
The sixth decade is coming to an end.
Doors have opened and shut.
The great distractions are over —
passion, children, the long indenture of marriage.
I fold them into a chest I will not take with me when I go.
Everyone says the world is flat and finite
on the other side of sixty.
That I will fall clear off the edge into darkness,
that no one will hear from me again
— or want to.
But I am ready for the knife slicing into the future,
for the quiet that explodes inside,
to join forces with the strong old woman,
to give everything away and begin again.
Now there is time to tell the story,
time to invent the new one —
to chain myself to a fence outside the missile base...
To pour my own blood on the walls of the Pentagon,
to walk a thousand miles with a begging bowl in my
hand.
There are places on this planet
where women past the menopause
put on tribal robes,
smoke pipes of wisdom — fly.

                                    by Marilyn Zukerman[15]

Here are some excerpts about the joys of remembering
that resonated with my own experience:

"Nothing will sharpen the memory, evoke the past, raise
the dead, rejuvenate the aging and cause both sighs and
smiles, like a collection of photographs gathered together
during the long years of life."[16]

At the time when my mother seemed near to dying, one
of my daughters put together a collage of photos from her
early childhood to her old age and mounted them on a

wooden board. My mother was too "far gone," to appreciate it, but the rest of the family vied to possess this treasure of memories. After that incident, it became a custom to make collages for other family members who died. Sometimes when a family holiday gets "sticky," we drag out the old albums for an instant mood-change and much nostalgia.

The intensity of the joy of remembering is increased in the company of another who shared the experience of the past. I love to meet a friend who lived in the same apartment building in New York City when I was 8 and she was 10. We both remember exactly what it was like to put the garbage into the dumbwaiter or to sunbathe on the filthy, tarred roof of that house each summer.

In a book about the Bronte family[17], it is said of the seventy-year-old father of the famous Emily and Charlotte, that:

"He had already entertained himself for a whole year by summoning ghosts...How fresh and hopeful the world had seemed when all whom he had known had been energetic. Ghostly, deceased clergymen moved about the air in Boundary Street like so many bats with smiling faces...with his inner eye he saw women who he had loved..."[18]

The heroine of a novel by Constance Beresford-Howe, *The Book of Eve*,[19] talks about forgetting and says:

"Forgot because I'm so busy remembering these days
— things and people now vanished like shadows on water, but still dimensional, moving around in a cinerama of memory. My father, for instance. He's been buried for thirty years now, but I was sure I saw him on the street the other day in his white scarf and long dark winter overcoat."[20]

Walking in the park the same heroine notices the people sitting on the benches: "They had the same look. Everyone who came to sit in the park had it: a look of experience completed. They were contemplatives; mystics. All a little crazy."[21] The image of the park-bench people was a happy one for me. It foreshadowed a time for myself, perhaps, where productivity and status wouldn't matter any more, only the joy of observing life and remembering.

In the novel *Mrs. Dalloway*, by Virginia Woolf, the heroine, asks her childhood friend:

"'Do you remember the lake?' she said, in an abrupt voice, under the pressure of an emotion which caught her heart, made the muscles of her throat stiff, and contracted her lips in a spasm as she said lake. For she was a child...and at the same time a grown woman coming to her parents who stood by the lake, holding her life in her arms which, as she neared them, grew larger and larger in her arms, until it became a whole life, a complete life, which she put down by them and said, 'This is what I have made of it! This!'"[22]

For me, this kind of joy comes often from pungent memories. I see a pattern on a dress, a certain striped T-shirt, red and white rows exactly the distance between them of a favorite polo-shirt I wore at camp as a kid. Completely distracted from, say, the Sunday liturgy, by the sight of this print on someone's shirt or dress, I will be wafted back to the smells and sounds of that YMCA camp years and years ago.

Ronald Blythe, author of *The View in Winter*, introduces some memories of old folk in rural England by a general observation about reminiscence. He claims that because elderly folk identify more with the past than the present, they are not attuned to the concerns of present-day politics in their town. Since their ethical views may also seem outdated to the young, they find it comforting to go back to a time when what they thought about life was not important: childhood.[23]

Blythe describes an old man going back to a task of the past, carving in wood as his father did when he was a boy, and feeling happier than he ever had in the previous decades of his life. Gardening plays a similar role in the lives of many others. Some enjoy being outdoors and free, even climbing apple trees which might be considered dangerous for an old one.

I find this to be true. I take even more joy than previously in my knitting and crocheting hobby. Before, I used to do this almost as occupational therapy amidst an overcrowded life, always combining my wool-work with visits, reading or TV. Now, I may sit for hours at a time making sweaters for members of my religious community by choice, without concern for the time element.

A new source of joy comes also from greater appreciation of small, good moments. I believe that the increase in gratitude for such little delights comes partly as a contrast to the pervading aches and pains. Thank God something good and pleasant is going on, I think, at least for a moment. Let me cherish this blessing before I am forced to attend to something painful.

Virginia Woolf describes her aging heroine believing that she scarcely needed the company of people anymore:

"Life itself, every moment of it, every drop of it, here, this instant...was enough. Too much indeed. A whole lifetime was too short to bring out, now that one had acquired the power, the full flavor; to extract every ounce of pleasure, every shade of meaning; when both were so much more solid than they used to be, so much less personal."[24]

Another of her characters reflects on how excited he can still be about sports scores. Peter Walsh is always reading about his favorite games:

"Having done things millions of times enriched them, though it might be said to take the surface off. The past enriched, and experienced, having cared for one or two people, and so having acquired the power which the young lack, of cutting short, doing what one likes, not caring a rap what people say and coming and going without any very great expectations..."[25]

This same character talks about the new power he has as an older man of taking hold of experience, of turning it round, slowly, in the light.

Another insight of Virginia Woolf is that when one was young, one was often too much excited to really know people.

I identified with Virginia Woolf's observation about older people liking to do repetitive things. I hated housework when it was part of a seemingly overwhelming burden of earning a living and taking care of children at the same time. Now, I find myself lulled into contentment by familiar tasks of folding wash, doing dishes, ironing clothes. Of course, now, there is no pressure.

Aging also has its own forms of humor. One of my favorite anecdotes of elderly humor comes from a book by two sisters in their hundreds, Bessie and Sadie Delaney, single, black, professional women:

"I'll tell you a story: The house we own is a two-family house, and sometimes the neighbors can hear us through the wall. One time, they had a guest who was up in arms. Just up in arms! She heard these sounds, like laughter, coming from outside, late at night, and she was convinced there were...ghosts. Our neighbor came over the next day and quizzed us down. And I said, 'Ain't no (ghosts), it's just the two of us being silly.' It hadn't occurred to them that these two old sisters, at our age, would be a-carrying on like that. I guess they think of old folks as people who sit around like old sourpusses. But not us. No, sir! When people ask me how we've lived past 100, I say, 'Honey, we never married. We never had husbands to worry us to death!'"[26]

The geriatric psychologist George Lawton writes about fresh joys coming from new goals. One of his maxims is that "We should seek not to add years to our life, but life to our years."[27] At this point in my life, which is more or less semi-retirement, since I am still pursuing my writing, if no longer a full-time professor and speaker, I find that a new project can bring an unexpected lift, particularly if it involves people with whom I enjoy working. I am getting tremendous happiness out of leading a writers' group, offering suggestions to others about their books in progress, helping them find publishing outlets. Sometimes I feel more excited about their books than my own.

A joy for some older people is to be able to mentor the young even in small ways. Living in an extended family with one of my daughters, son-in-law, and grandchildren, it is usually I who need the help of the others, but sometimes a child will come running to me in my little suite, "Daddy wants to know where the fabric store is?" Yes, I know. I can help out! Better still, if the question is about some religious concept or fact.

I came across a humorous but telling old Balinese legend about essential mentoring:

Once upon a time a tribe in a remote village used to sacrifice and then eat their old men. Finally, all the traditions were lost because there was not a single old man around. The group was building a big meeting house. They had a pile of tree-trunks ready but no one could tell how to place them. If the timber were placed the wrong way up, it would lead to disastrous consequences. The project came to a halt until a young man said he would produce an old man if they promised not to eat any old men again. They promised. He brought his grandfather, whom he had hidden; and the old man taught the community to tell top from bottom.

As I ponder the new joys of aging described in this section, I pray:

Lord, let me not miss any joys because of the self-absorbed, problem-oriented contraction of my spirit I get involved in so often. Please, God, show me what you are trying to give me.

FOR PERSONAL REFLECTION AND GROUP SHARING:
1. What are your favorite things to reminisce about from the past? Childhood, teens, young adult years, work, family, friends, volunteering, church?
2. What are the small gifts of life you cherish now?
3. What are some humorous moments of your aging experience? (One reader of a draft of this book said — the most humorous part is that I don't even think I'm aging!)
4. Does anyone in the family, neighborhood or church seek you out for help or mentoring?

Loneliness and Closeness

"It is not good for man to be alone." (Gen. 2:18)

As a widow, when I think of closeness and loneliness, the first thing that comes to mind is spousal love or lack of it; family or lack of it. My research taught me to think in broader terms. Read this poem, for instance. Isn't there a special kind of closeness that exists even between a spectator and the people she or he looks at:

"I like the sound
of old women
marching to church,
or crackling grocery bags...
I like the sound of old women
talking
loudly to old men,
softly to newborns,
gently to young marrieds,
planning lives and death..."

by Mary Sue Koeppel[28]

I asked a man who had just enjoyed this poem what would be a masculine equivalent. He said that he loved to watch old Italian men playing bocci.

Then there is a closeness of people who have lived a long time in a neighborhood. Even if they do not know each other intimately, may not even have been inside each other's houses, they may feel they belong together. In Bennett's novel, *The Old Wives' Tale,* we become acquainted with Sophia, an Englishwoman who has been running a boarding house in Paris for 25 years. The narrator suggests that:

"There was nothing to prevent her going back to (her small town in England). No, nothing except the fact that her whole soul recoiled from the mere idea of any such enterprise! She was a fixture in the Rue Lord Byron. She was a part of the street. She knew all that happened or could happen there. She was attached to it by heavy chains of habit. There! The incandescent gas-burner of the street-lamp outside had been turned down, as it was turned down, every night!...That phenomenon was a portion of her life, dear to her."[29]

When my mother was in her eighties, in preparation for a move to a residence apartment smaller than the cluttered one in which she had spent the previous ten years, I was helping her get rid of many of her furnishings. Stuffing things that would be junk to me into large, black, plastic garbage bags, I was gleeful. But she was crestfallen. In an unusually quiet tone of voice she remarked: "When you live alone, your things become like friends, Ronda." In my late forties, then, I didn't understand. Now in my sixties, I do. I love to return to my cell-like rooms below the main stories of my daughter's house just to be able to gaze at pictures that have lasted for decades, a candelabra bought in Sicily in the days when my husband and I were engaged. I don't often feel lonely in these rooms because they are filled with these material "friends."

In the book *The View in Winter* there was discussion of another form of loneliness — not the kind that comes from lacking close family connections — but simply a distancing coming from manifold generation gaps. This feeling is reported by a man in his eighties interviewed by Ronald Blythe:

"I am not going to say that my generation was better than any other generation, but somehow it seems that we were a little bit on the plus side. If only because so many of us kept so well in our later years. We were a pretty good breed! A good vintage. But now I feel I am in a stranger's world. It is a feeling which increases day by day. I'm a conservative but I'm not a hide-bound conservative. In fact, I once voted Labour, so I'm not a reactionary. But I feel a bit isolated now — very much so, in fact. I don't like what is going on all around me. One of the reasons why I wouldn't care if somebody told me, 'Well, you've only got a couple of years left,' is that I don't feel as though I belong here anymore."[30]

It seems that there is less of a generation gap, or what is now called a disconnect, when younger members of the family think of their elders as wise counselors. But even if there are times of need where a young person will turn to parents or grandparents, there are still certain times when the gap is felt keenly. In my case, this happens when a large group of younger family members get together for holidays. Many of them are computer experts and they can talk for hours in abbreviations and catch-phrases I can't understand at all. Then there might be discs playing for hours and hours — songs they all loved when they were teens — songs I never knew.

The interview with the old man from the book *The View in Winter*, continues on:

"I always regret my age because there were so many things I could do and I can't do now. But if there's not much physical satisfaction, there's still a great mental satisfaction. Sometimes I get, well, I shouldn't call it a superiority complex, but a pleasure, because I can go back further than somebody else and say, 'I was there, I saw it.' They would know nothing whatever of things I actually saw and did. That does give me a bit of satisfaction. Nothing shocks you, but they don't understand this. Unless you're a bloody idiot, if you've lived for eighty years you must know *something*! But for some reason you're not supposed to know what you know, or what the young know. But you do...That is why it is bitter to be old."[31]

I have come to realize that the desire for intimate relationships varies greatly among the aging. Many widows say that they have not the slightest wish to remarry. Others at any age hope above all else for a new spouse. I am impressed by the way Virginia Woolf describes the yearning for romantic love and the surprise others may find in hearing of it. The hero of *Mrs. Dalloway*, Peter Walsh, is in his fifties. Old enough for that era. He is thinking of marrying a very young woman with two children. Peter tells his childhood friend, Clarissa, about this new romance. She is appalled that he at his age should be sucked under by such passion when "his neck is scrawny and his hands are red." She thinks it great egotism for someone that age to think a young woman would love him. But yet, the very thought of his passion makes her feel young and tremulous.

My experience is that there are people of eighty who can still be madly in love. Younger people may think it odd, or pathetic, or even crazed, but that might be a judgement they don't need to make at all. Even if the main form of closeness we crave is gentle companionship, there may still be moments when Eros reasserts itself, as explained in this poem, written by a woman but equally applicable to older men:

Spring Surge
My blood still answers to the hawk's wild cry,
Although my years are many, and the fine,
Clean edge of passion dulled by long disuse.

Love now is gentler. And the more diffuse
Emotion of compassion is most often mine.
Yet in me passion's remnants will not die."

                                        by Kay Loftus[32]

A male reader of this book in draft was surprised this poem wasn't by a man since he identified with it so much in a masculine way.

For me, such moments of passion occur primarily when I think, out of illusion, that some man of the past I once loved might be interested in me as "more than a friend." I have come to see that such a thought sets off a cycle of feelings: wishes, resignation, melancholy, what if? Finally, I realize that even if one of these men were serious, my deepest wish is to belong to Christ as a nun.

On the other side, there are women who feel so badly about their physical appearance that they don't even want closeness. Do you shudder, as I did, reading this description by Virginia Woolf of a woman "feeling herself suddenly shriveled, aged, breastless"?[33]

On a softer note, from a widow:
"After Elbert went upstairs, I was lonesome.
I got me a road dog with fleas and a porch dog,
but didn't get no bed dog. Didn't want to give
up the quiet after Elbert's snoring stopped.
Some things about him I miss, but that's private."[34]

Most of us, perhaps because of growing physical weakness and vulnerability in aging, long most of all for tenderness. In "A Living Will," Naomi Halperin Spigle writes about her hopes for the very end of her life:
"When they say I cannot
hear you, sing me lullabies
and folk songs, the ones
I sang to you. I will hear them
as an unborn child can hear
its mother's music through

the waters of the womb...
When they tell you
to go home, stay with me
if you can. Deep
inside I will be
weeping."[35]
Relationships of the elderly to grandchildren or the off-
spring of friends can be particularly tender:
"It was an old, old, old, old lady,
And a boy that was half past three;
And the way that they played together
Was beautiful to see."

by Henry Cuyler Bunner[36]
Part of any discourse about the experiences of closeness
and solitude during the later years of life must be life-style
issues. Should all aging people try to be part of an extended
family? Is it better, if you are not married, to adjust to living
with one old friend, or are there benefits to trying to go it
alone? Does institutional living have to be a nightmare?
What about setups like retirement hotels or assisted living
arrangements where a couple can live together? Or how
about a colony of retired people living in trailers by the
beach in a resort town, having fun together sitting outside in
the evenings? I would like to share some thought-provoking
excerpts.

Let me start with a funny one. A teacher asks a child to
write about Christmas vacation. Here is that youngster's humorous description of a visit to a retirement colony to spend
time with elderly relatives:
"We always used to spend Christmas with Grandpa
and Grandma. They used to live here, in a big brick
house, but Grandpa got retarded and they moved to
Florida. Now they live in a place with a lot of other
retarded people. They all live in little tin boxes. They
ride three-wheeled tricycles and they all wear name

tags because they don't know who they are all the
time. They go to a big building called a wrecked hall,
but if it was wrecked, they got it fixed because it is all
right now. They play games and do exercises there,
but they don't do them very good. There is a swimming pool there. They go into it and just stand there
with their hats on. I guess they don't know how to
swim.

As you go in their park, there is a doll house with a
little man sitting in it. He watches all day so that they
can't get out without him seeing them. When they
sneak out they go to the beach and pick up shells.

My Grandma used to bake cookies and stuff, but I
guess she forgot how. Nobody cooks, they just eat
out. They eat the same thing every night called early
birds. Some of the people are so retarded that they
don't know how to cook at all, so my Grandma and
Grandpa bring food into the wrecked hall and they
call it potluck.

Grandma says Grandpa worked all his life and earned
his retardment. I wish they would move back up here.
I guess the man in the doll house won't let them out."

On a more serious note, a comment about the downside
of what is called being a snowbird came to my attention. In
case you don't know this term, a "snowbird" is one who
regularly migrates south from cold Northern climes, spending often 6 months every year in a trailer park or fancier
dwelling enjoying the sun. A snowbird friend of mine whom
I see only in the winter where I live in Arizona mentioned
one liability of this seemingly idyllic life-style for the retired. "There's no continuity. By now my old friends from
Minnesota have become slightly colder to me each time I
come back full of tales of my paradise in Arizona. And my
new friends down South get really put out when I am off
again to the North for a six month vacation in the summer!"

A solution to this dilemma was suggested by a friend who told of groups of "snowbirds" who migrate as a clan from New Jersey to Florida every year.

If deluxe retirement villages and snow-bird colonies seem idyllic as future possibilities, at least to visitors, the mood that comes upon those contemplating convalescent homes or wards is much darker. Even before such a move seems necessary there is fear: of loss of memory, of wards in hospitals with long rows of frighteningly out of it old folks. In the past there were usually women at home to look after the elderly, but now most of these women are out at work with no time to care for anyone.

A contrast can be found in the attitude of a woman from rural England described by Blythe in *The View in Winter*. She reports that taking care of her old husband was actually a maturing experience. "I was shy as a child," she said. But now she doesn't hold back because she has to speak up for her husband. She thinks generations of families (like the poor refugees) should all live under one roof. Talking about the workhouses where they took old people to die, she re-marks that "I never want to finish my time in them places. I've got such a willpower, I'll keep goin'"[37]

Here is a heartwarming story, also from *The View in Winter*, about closeness under conditions that could be daunting: Colonel Hardy, S.A., 75, was in the Salvation Army and was used to lots of action. When it came time to retire, it was a shock to move from a life geared to action and self-less involvement, to lots of time to brood about himself. Blythe remarks that upon retirement there emerges an unfamiliar and usually unattractive self. Part of the task of the elderly person is to come to grips with this reality. The transition for Colonel Hardy was facilitated by getting close to a widow who was also miserable and lonely.

Sick of her own morbid grief after the death of her first husband, the widow decided that God was fed up with her because she had turned down all his sensible solutions for her life. Then it seemed that God said: "There are a lot of dreary old women like you. Go and do some work, you are as strong as a horse still. How about reading to the blind? Something like that?" So, she obeyed God and met Colonel Hardy who was going blind. They eventually married in spite of the Colonel's fears that he was worthless because of his disability. The widow is deeply in love with her second husband.

Blythe includes an interesting note about the blindness the Colonel experienced.

"He is not in blackness, he says, he is in an object-less light, opalescent and restful. He has no intention of ever reading Braille, because he has no intention of ever reading or writing again...the pictures in his mind have been sharpened by his sightlessness into an iridescence which has retrieved every sight and sound he experienced (in the past)."[38]

The old Colonel also talked to Blythe about old age in Africa, where he was once stationed, in contrast to English life. There is a great deal of respect and reverence for the elderly in Africa, he said. "But old age in England is just a social nuisance. I saw some boys talking about an old man when he was struggling onto a bus, say they thought he should be shot! The old man turned to the lads and said, 'Be careful, you could be shot when *you* get to seventy!'"[39]

Nonetheless, even when grown children say they want to care for their old folk, the elderly persons might be thinking that it is more charitable to save their adult children from that burden. Sometimes a couple is divided as they consider future possibilities for themselves. One may be thinking about the graces their children will receive in the process of lovingly caring for them until the end. His or her spouse can-

not bear the idea of becoming a wretched old creature
in need of the must humiliating services.

More about this in the section of professional wisdom
about aging.

I want to end this chapter about loneliness and closeness
with a poem my mother wrote in the final decade of her life:

OLD AND ALONE
Without love
She said
The flesh shrivels
The mind dulls
The heart dies
But, my dear,
This is the human condition
At your time of life
You know that.
You must turn to God.
He alone is always there
And loves you.
Yes — ah, yes — God
But
God has no arms to put around me
No hands to clasp in mine or stroke my hair
No chest on which to rest my head
No wit to set my mind to dancing
No sudden smile to pierce my heart with love
No lips to kiss
No body to join with mine in union...
Don't you see? Don't you understand?
I am drowning in a sea of loneliness
I need a living, breathing human being
To love and call my own.
You long for what you can no longer have
Take pleasure in what you still have left...
Eyes to see the lovely light of sun on grass

Ears to hear the music of a child's laugh
Pass along a word of wisdom to one who needs it
Hold a sobbing child to your breast...
You supply to someone else the very things you miss.
Give your arms, your hands, your wit, your smile.
A close embrace to warm another's frozen soul.
Revive another's dying heart.
It is the lonely who must help the lonely.
by Helen Winner
A prayer about loneliness and human company:
Dear Lord, we know in the depths of our souls that we
are never alone because You are always with us. But
sometimes our hearts quake with loneliness, with
yearning for purely human contact. And sometimes
by contrast, we feel suffocated, surrounded by people
we are not close to. Help us to find You in our fear.
Help us to trust that you will bring those to us who
can help us most to grow in love.

FOR PERSONAL REFLECTION AND GROUP SHARING:

1. How do you feel about being alone in the last years of your life?
2. With what people do you feel the greatest closeness as you age?
3. How do you think you want to live at different stages you might anticipate in your own aging process?
4. Can you think of negative and positive examples you have witnessed yourself of living situations for the elderly?
5. You might want to write a page describing a perfect day in your life as you think it might be 10 years from now. Include the people you would like to have with you. The writing may help you plan for the future. If you are sharing in a group, what ideas of the others would you want to include in your life ten years from now?

Physical Pain

"Take pity on me, Yahweh,
I am in trouble now.
Grief wastes away my eye,
My throat, my inmost parts.
For my life is worn out with sorrow,
my years with sighs;
my strength yields under misery,
my bones are wasting away.
I am contemptible,
Loathsome to my neighbors,
to my friends a thing of fear.
Those who see me in the street
hurry past me;
I am forgotten, as good as dead in their hearts,
something discarded." (Psalm 31:9-12)

There are many kinds of physical suffering connected with aging: fatigue, chronic, low level aches, greater pains connected with various illnesses or disabilities; sharp pain that cannot be medicated without worse side-effects.

Besides conditions of the present, there is also the fear of living with such problems in the future. We all know that many of our illnesses or disabilities of today usually lead to other pains in the future. We hear about what others are suffering and worry that these ailments will come to us, if not soon, then later on, should we be so fortunate or unfortunate as to live much longer.

In this section about what aging feels like, I am not going to make an exhaustive list of physical discomforts and pains. Such inventories can only be depressing. Instead, I would like to relay a few sample anecdotes to indicate to the reader that his or her experience is not isolated.

How about myself? Well, as of the present I am suffering from long-term effects of a previous seemingly successful mastectomy: chronic back problems, hemorrhoids, bleeding gums and sporadic toothache. Not too bad, but enough to make a painless day unlikely. Yearly check-ups for cancer with the discovery of maybe malignant tumors do nothing to make a woman confident. I realize that I am relatively lucky, especially when reading an account like the following from *The View in Winter.* A Lieutenant, age 84, wounded in WWI shares with Blythe, the interviewer:

"I've had pain and inconvenience from the War for close on sixty years. I am deaf and my wounds still hurt so badly that I have to recite poetry to myself to get to sleep. I would never take a drug and I'm not the sort to make a prayer, so I say these poems in the dark when my leg hurts. This wretched knee of mine keeps me awake, year after year, and I recite hundreds and hundreds of lines of poetry to keep my mind off it. I usually start off with Gray's Elegy. I find that very soothing, very pain-alleviating. I like that poem more and more. Then Dryden and Pope and Kipling — On the Road to Mandalay — oh, a very mixed bag indeed! Shakespeare, of course.

In hospital, just after the First World War, I was immobilized for many months. I couldn't do a thing for myself, so I learnt long passages of Shakespeare by heart and said them to myself. That is how it started. It gave me an enormous amount of pleasure. I find that reciting poetry when you have pain and can't sleep is something between an anodyne and a prayer...

And I'm deaf. This ear went first because it was damaged when I was blown up at the front. The deafness increases slowly and inexorably. They tell me that when I am ninety I won't hear anything at all. Silence. But I haven't heard the kind of talk you get at ordinary social gatherings for a long time. You're apt to guess at what people say and it makes you look a little

senile. But I'm not senile. It is just that at parties and
things you've got no sense of direction. It makes it
very tricky. It has made me a fireside man now, un-
doubtedly a fireside man now. I resent these disabilities — when I remember them! But when a man's
very old, all kinds of abnormalities become very normal, you know. You can't help being old. You can't
help being any age. Here I am, near eighty-five, and I
can't help that!

I don't regret the War in spite of hospital and all the
rest of it. When I joined up I was a diffident, bookish
young man, the worst possible mixer. The army
brought me out and eventually it gave me a tremendous amount of confidence. I was proud that I'd managed to get an external honors degree, but I soon
found that in the army there were all kinds of aca-
demically deprived men who were better people than
I was. And that many drunken officers were braver
than I was, when it came to it. I was terrified of so
many things and I met men who were frightened of
nothing. Of course, we all put on a bit of a show to
hide that we didn't need to put on a bit of a show. If
you get me."[40]

"...You hear old men say that their bodies have become a burden to them. My body became a burden to
me when I was twenty-four, but I wouldn't say that I
found it a burden now. It is very far from being a burden. Because it hampered me so much when it should
not have done — when I was young — I hardly think
of it at all now...

The War clings to me. The other day, while driving
my car with my leg bent up, I felt a small, hard, rough
scrap of something between my knee and my trou-
sers. Another bit of shrapnel had worked its way
out."[41]

Closer to home, here are some excerpts from the thoughts of two contemporary American writers concerning the physical miseries of aging. From Shelby Foote at age 61: "There's not only no place I want to see; even if I wanted to see it, I wouldn't go."[42] He feels his body dwindling as if his selfhood was "tied to a dying animal."

The novelist Walker Percy says that in his sixties he was feeling "shaky, seedy, molted, unfit, with no stomach for tackling anything."[43]

In the same book containing letters sent by these writers to each other, Foote remarks about an acquaintance of theirs: first he "couldn't leave town, then the block, then the house, then his room, and finally, I guess, his bed."[44]

A dear friend of mine here in Arizona, Dr. Elizabeth Valerius, a psychotherapist, described to me her feelings about a terrible bout with disabling rheumatoid arthritis. Because she suffered from pulmonary disorders as a child she had learned to take pain as part of life, but nothing could compare to this onslaught of pain at the age of sixty-eight. The arthritis pain was excruciating and permeated her entire body such that even with codeine every two and a half hours she was hardly able to move out of her bed. The isolation was one of the worst elements of this ailment. Knowing that her father had lived into his late eighties and her mother to one hundred and one she began to wish she could leave "this life plane" sooner rather than later, especially finding it intolerable to be alive and not able to be of service to anyone else.

Believing that God could lift this pain in one second caused something of a crisis in faith as she would wonder why God didn't work a miracle for her. During this period, now on the way to remission, hopefully, Elizabeth understood how bitter someone could become in such a state. How easy it would be to sink into permanent invalidism, to stay in bed and let others take care of her or even become institutionalized. When one is in such pain and under medication it seems too much of an effort to make decisions or do anything.

Now that her pain has abated Elizabeth realizes that she can make much use of the years that remain and find them a blessing she would not have experienced so keenly had she not gone through those years of misery. Now even when the pain returns she doesn't let it stop her from living, patiently doing the exercises recommended to build up her body. She is using her talents as a therapist to help many friends, and also new clients. She also recognizes those terrible years of suffering were partly related to anxiety experienced from years of nursing her father, husband, and mother in their last years.

Here is a prayer you might say to express your feelings about physical pain:

"Jesus, I know that when you suffered on earth, you included all our pain in yours. Let me never think of myself as alone with my suffering. Help me to offer up my pain with yours for the redemption of the world."

FOR PERSONAL REFLECTION AND GROUP SHARING:
1. Make a list of the physical pains you experience including fatigue, chronic pain, and sharp pain you can't medicate without bad side-effects. Make a list also of the types of pain you fear the most.
2. Give each pain you feel to Christ. Imagine Him by your side carrying the yoke of pain with you.
3. Write a prayer you might want to say now or in the future, offering up each type of pain for intentions of your choice.

Approaching Death

"Some deadly thing has fastened upon him:
he will not rise again from where he lies." (Psalm 41:15-16)

In later chapters I will be writing extensively about the Christian approach to death. There we will see clearly how different it is to approach death with the hope of eternal life (as most religious people do) than it is for one whose horizons are limited to this world.

That contrast is especially real to me because of my personal history. I was raised as an atheist with no conception of anything to follow biological death. Whenever I thought about death, before my conversion, I felt terrible fear. My consciousness to be snuffed out! Horrible! Now as a Christian I am full of hope, looking forward to death as a release into the joys of union with God.

But right now, in this chapter, I want to reflect on the approach of death as those do who have either only a foggy idea of eternity or who are convinced there is no life after death. If you are a believer in life after death, you may identify with some of these excerpts just the same. Why? Because they resonate with our own feelings at times of doubt and despair.

Let's consider our old friend Virginia Woolf's Mrs. Dalloway. Generally a cheerful soul, in the midst of hostessing a brilliant party, a shadow falls over her contentment:

> "When she was younger it would have intoxicated her to have other people so delighted by her party. But now it all had a hollowness; at arm's length they were, not in the heart; and it might be that she was growing old but they satisfied her no longer as they used to. She, an atheist, sees how death was there in waiting. Beneath the chatter, lies...one was alone."[45]

Or listen to the voice of a gentleman interviewed by Blythe in *The View in Winter*:

> "I'm no good at what they call the 'eternal.' Some old people say that they are approaching it or have a belief that they are coming to it, but I don't. I feel I

should, but I don't. I feel I want to make my peace, but with what, with whom? I'm not a religious man. I was, in upbringing, but most of it has vanished. I go to church occasionally and observe the conventions, but I don't devote any thought to faith. It is not a big feature with me. My education apart, I am a villager — fatalistic, you know. It all comes out at the end. You know what you *don't* believe, when you're in your eighties."[46]

Depressing? I think so. But there can be a worldly sense of death that is not so grim. Some even think of it with humor. I find this poem of Ellen Kort amazing:

If Death Were a Woman
"I'd want her to come for me smelling of cinnamon
wearing bright cotton purple maybe hot pink
she would not bathe me Instead we'd scrub the porch
pour leftover water on flowers stand a long time
in sun and silence then holding hands
we'd pose for pictures in the last light"[47]

In the same book, *I am Becoming the Woman I've Wanted*, there is a description by Ruth Moose of an old woman who was a teetotaler most of her life but in great old age liked to drink blackberry wine. "Death found she was not afraid, took her hand. At ninety-three she knew she couldn't outbluff him, so she went calling her greeting ahead."[48]

Yet, many others are afraid, if not of death, of the approach of death.

"We wonder how much older we have to become, and what degree of decay we may have to endure. We keep whispering to ourselves, 'Is this age yet? How far must I go?' For age can be dreaded more than death...It is waiting for death that wears us down, and the distaste for what we may become."[49]

"What does it feel like to be nearly a hundred years old?" The shepherd's widow was asked, by Blythe. She was stout and sane. "Well, you wake up in the morning, you say to yourself, "What, still here?"[50]

My prayer about approaching death is this:

Thank you, Jesus, for the way you have intertwined fear of death with hope of glorious happiness for those who put their trust in you. Let me not linger on feelings natural to all of us, but inappropriate to those who know about You. When such resigned or despairing feelings about death come, let me turn to You and Your word for a different story.

FOR PERSONAL REFLECTION AND GROUP SHARING:
1. Trace your concept and feeling about death from childhood to the present.
2. Do you have trouble believing in eternal life?

Heroes and Heroines of Aging

*"You shall come to your grace in ripe old age, as a shock of grain comes
up to the threshing floor in its season."* (Job 5:26)

During one of my workshops on aging, a woman came forward during a break to challenge me. "You're making this seem like a down-hill road. Why don't you talk more about heroes and heroines of aging — all those marvelous women and men who defy the stereotype?"

I replied, "I guess I'm afraid if I talked too much about these giants, people who are struggling with aging would feel like failures!"

There was no time for further conversation at the workshop, but the phrase remained in my mind. "Heroes and heroines of aging." Did the thought of people like Gandhi or Eleanor Roosevelt, Pablo Casals or Grandma Moses really make me feel like a failure? When I read about them, don't I rather take hope that I too might someday be strong and wise, especially if I didn't give in to fatigue and discouragement?

Of course, in my list of heroes and heroines of aging there would be many canonized saints. The story of how they aged I had planned to include from the start of my research. Their lives and wisdom in aging was to be the climax of my book. You will find them under the last section of this book: Wisdom of the Church.

Heroes and heroines of aging? Matching these words were many people of my own acquaintance who had amazed me by their energy all the way through their eighties and even nineties. An old mystic still reading Scripture and dispensing holy thoughts in his 99th year: my mentor Charles Rich. A woman in her nineties radiating love and gratitude from her bed in a convalescent home by whose side was her husband, a philosophy professor, writing thoughts about gratitude until his last day: my godparents, Leni and Balduin Schwarz. A seventy-year-old who can hike and bike for hours, drives six hours within a day back and forth bringing clothing and other supplies to the Missionaries of Charity in a distant city: Evie Brandin. A Catholic intellectual crusader, on fire with love for the Church until his last days: Dietrich Von Hildebrand. A single woman who adopted nine children from many lands and home-schooled them while being a full-time professor: Yvonne Rosedale. It would have been significant for me also to have met someone like the famous old Chasidic Rabbi of Brooklyn who was reputed to be so holy that he was judged as a Messiah figure.

Perhaps even more touching of the elderly of my own acquaintance were friends whose faults seemed to dissolve as they aged so that they became holy in and through physical weakness. The thought of these beloved older friends, now gone on to eternity, does not serve to make me feel inadequate. They seem more like "pace-makers," pushing me to better hope.

Before describing in some details the last part of the lives of figures well-known to the whole world, I want to mention a few that have come up recently.

The cover story of Parade Magazine in 1993 tells of one Corena Leslie of Peoria, Arizona, skydiving just 3 days before her 90th birthday. Her face is lit up — almost ecstatic — with a huge grin.[51] Editions of the same magazine in 1998,[52] highlight Dodo Cheney, winner of 286 U.S. Tennis Association titles, who still competes at 81; Harry Belafonte, still singing and acting at 71; Clint Eastwood, acting and directing at 67; and business executives still going strong in their 60's and up. John Glenn thrilled the nation by going up into space once more at the age of seventy-seven.

These athletic feats reminded me of a segment on television about a team of mountain-climbers who included an elderly woman. The rules of the competition were such that the whole group would fail if one member had to drop out along the many day route. Nonetheless, this team decided to take the risk of losing for the greater gain of watching the intrepid progress of one who refused to give up just because of age.

A best-selling book about how a particular individual faced impending death from Lou Gehrig's disease, *Tuesdays with Morrie*, was made into a book-tape.[53] Listening to the account about Morrie Schwartz, a sociology professor at Brandeis, by his former student Mitch Albom, certain words of wisdom stood out for me:

"I mourn the dwindling time but I am glad of the time to make things right."

"Always get the most out of life; give the most love possible."

"Without love you have broken wings."

"Love or die, be compassionate."

"To be every age now, because you know all ages now."
"To accept the dependency that comes with the last illness — to be taken care of as in babyhood. You give as an adult, but you have to take as a child."
Many there are among famous people whose aging was memorable. I can only include a few examples here. You can make note of your own favorites as you respond to the questions for personal reflection and group sharing.

Mohandas K. Gandhi, died at 79 in 1948. He was called Mahatma — which means "great soul," in Hindi. Living in terms of his ideals of non-violence it seems natural that he thought of strength not in terms of physical capacity but rather in terms of "an indomitable will."

Conquering the anxiety that comes with a life of politics through serenity of soul certainly had a lot to do with Gandhi's faith in God. He thought that belief in God was more real than life itself.[54]

At the end of his life, his voice was gentle and sweet yet still carried far. He spoke slowly and precisely, like a child. He used to say that the proof that his spiritual method worked would be how he would respond if assassinated — always a possibility in his troubled country. In fact, when he was shot to death the words he said meant, "I forgive you, I love you, I bless you."[55]

On My Own is a book Eleanor Roosevelt wrote about her life after the death of FDR.[56] Eleanor died at 78 in 1962. I remember always thinking of her as a kind of Amazon of strength for keeping up work on social action projects all over the world way into old age. Whatever a reader might think of her policies, what she says about being a widow is significant for this book.

Eleanor thought that you begin to die when you stop doing helpful things for others. But it is important to do things you really believe personally to be important vs. things others expect of you:

"(after the death of FDR) I had few definite plans but I knew there were certain things I did not want to do. I did not want to run an elaborate household again...the fact that I kept myself well occupied made my loneliness less acute...my philosophy has been that if you have work to do and do it to the best of your ability you will not have so much time to think about yourself."[57]

Pablo Casals, the famous Spanish cellist, manifests certain features of aging I found intriguing. About a late marriage to a much younger woman he used to say that it didn't matter what others thought of them: "They cannot know our happiness." Another, seemingly trivial, but perhaps really important aspect of his later life was interest in hobbies. From childhood he included tennis, horseback riding, and playing dominoes in between his grueling schedule of cello practice. This he thought necessary for balance. In his nineties Casals still enjoyed playing games. He did not like the concept of retirement. The idea was alien to him because his work as a musician was his life. Each day one must be reborn and begin ones work again. "I could not betray my old friend, the cello."

The opening sentence of the book *Joys and Sorrows: Reflection of Pablo Casals*, reads:

"On my last birthday I was ninety-three years old. That is not young, of course...but age is a relative matter. If you continue to work and to absorb the beauty in the world about you, you find that age does not necessarily mean getting old. At least, not in the ordinary sense. I feel many things more intensely than ever before, and for me life grows more fascinating."[58]

Grandma Moses (1860-1961), the famous American painter, is a figure who has haunted me because her success came at such a late age.[59] A farm girl from upstate New York, Grandma Moses used to paint more or less as a hobby

on wallpaper, masonite, etc. When she was in her late seventies, a painting of hers was seen in the window of a drug-
store by a man who bought up everything she had and
launched her in the New York art world. Asked in a TV interview what she was going to do for the next twenty years,
she pointed up and said, "I am going up yonder." I was
amused to learn that she danced a jig on her 100th birthday.

A prayer about heroes and heroines of aging:
There are flashy ways of standing out as an elderly
person. Perhaps some people admire me as a hero or
heroine of aging for some achievement visible to all.
Perhaps not. I know that in your eyes the only thing
that counts is being a hero or heroine of love. Show
me how to use my gifts, talents and even weaknesses
to glorify you at this time in my life.

FOR PERSONAL REFLECTION AND GROUP SHARING:
　1. Who are your heros and heroines of aging from among
　　　people you have known personally?
　2. What people known to many do you think of as heroes and
　　　heroines of aging?
　3. What characteristics or wisdom of the heroes and heroines
　　　I have chronicled especially challenged you?

WISDOM FROM THE PROFESSIONALS

"When wisdom comes into your heart
and knowledge is a delight to you
then prudence will be there to watch over you,
and discernment be your guardian..." (Proverbs 2:10-11)

When I first started working on this book it was to be sub-titled "The Wisdom of the Word vs. the Wisdom of the Saints." But once I got into my research on secular ideas about aging I had to do an about-face. What became clear is that even if I might disagree with the over-all outlook of many non-religious writers, what most of them had to say about aging was right on.

So I got rid of the sub-title contrasting worldly and Christian wisdom to emphasize, instead, the way the real wisdom of the Church takes up where the real wisdom of the professionals leaves off. Often times, as you will see, the wisdom of the world not only does not contradict spiritual wisdom but even points toward it.

Those of you who are experts on the wisdom of the professional concerning aging may feel frustrated with this section. Not being an expert in the field of geriatrics from any point of view, all I was able to do was to summarize and comment upon certain truths that came my way. In the sections for personal reflection and group sharing there will be plenty of room for your greater knowledge and insight.

Wisdom from Literature

One of the most intriguing thoughts about aging I found in my readings was this one from the French writer La Rochefoucauld:

"Few people know how to be old."[60]

What can that mean? One of the reasons I love to include literary images from others in my own books is because elegantly expressed images about life force us to think. I'm not sure what this remark meant to its author. To me it conveys the possibility that aging might be an art and that learning this art might enhance my life in ways I cannot predict.

Evidently Ronald Blythe, the sociologist I have borrowed from so much already, also finds literature to be a source of truth. He includes many literary images in his book, *The View in Winter*. Let me share my favorites.

Blythe likes the concept of aging manifested by Chaucer in his famous saga *The Canterbury Tales*. An old woman in one of the Tales "reared chickens —and was content with her lot, her diet kept healthy by a narrow purse, her body exercised by hard work and, now and then, a jolly dance, there was little to fear. No gout, no apoplexy and nothing ridiculous or repellent for the world to condemn."[61]

A lovely line from Shakespeare goes, "In winter's tedious nights sit by the fire with good old folks and let them tell you tales." Shakespeare sometimes like to mock old men who refused to age with dignity. Falstaff is questioned by a friendly scoffer:

"Have you not a moist eye, a dry hand, a yellow cheek, a white beard, a decreasing leg, an increasing belly? Is not your voice broken, your wind short, your chin double, your wit single, and every part of you blasted with antiquity? And will you yet call yourself young? Fie, fie, fie, Sir John!"[62]

In the play King Lear, however, we get a full, serious

treatment of the problems of aging. Reading that famous play as a young girl, I had no use for old Lear, being much more interested in his daughters. Rereading the play at sixty, though, I was fascinated by the universality of the plight of Lear. How many older parents groaning under the weight of doubts about the loyalty of their off-spring, seek to manipulate those sons and daughters into assuming unwelcome roles for their own benefit? How many older folk also learn like Lear to be endlessly grateful for real love and affection given in spite of their many faults? And, in the end, may we not echo these lines of Lear: "To shake all cares and business from our age, conferring them on younger strengths, while we unburdened crawl toward death."[63]

This line from Goethe's *Faust* about living out our years on earth in the light of our eternal destiny has always been a favorite of mine:

"All that is but transitory (on earth) is only an image...of eternity."

The poetic line is made even more fullsome in expressiveness by the famous musical passage based on it to be found in Mahler's Eighth Symphony.

In quite a different mood is this poem of Philip Larkin quoted by Blythe:

"Be your age — not looking forward or back.
Always too eager for the future, we
Pick up bad habits of expectancy."
— and —
"You cannot always keep
that unfakable
That unfakable young surface.
You must learn your lines."[64]

To me, this poet's voice was chiding. It challenged me to throw off such silly forms of regression as imagining I can appear to be much younger than I am. The mirror can't be that wrong! Or, again, don't I feel better as a dignified,

amused spectator at a party than as a laughing hyena?
How pathetic but true is this poem?
"I used to think that grown-up people chose
To have stiff backs and wrinkles round their nose,
and veins like small fat snakes on either hand,
On purpose to be grand.
Till through the banisters I watched one day
My great-aunt Etty's friend who was going away,
And how her onyx beads had come unstrung.
I saw her grope to find them as they rolled;
And then I knew that she was helplessly old,
As I was helplessly young."
Frances Cornford[65]
Chilling indeed this Auden commentary:
Old People's Home
...The elite can dress and decent themselves,
are ambulant with a single stick, adroit
to read a book all through, or play the slow movements of
easy sonatas...
Then come those on wheels, the average
majority, who endure T.V. and, led by
lenient therapists, do community singing, then
the loners, muttering in Limbo, and last
the terminally incompetent, as impeccable,
improvident, unspeakable as the plants
they parody. (Plants may sweat profusely but never
sully themselves.) One tie, thought unites them: all
appeared when the world, though much was awry
there, was more
spacious, more comely to look at, its Old Ones
with an audience and secular station. (Then a child,
in dismay with Mamma, could refuge with Gran
to be revalued and told a story.) As of now,
we all know what to expect, but their generation

is the first to fade like this, not at home but assigned
to a numbered frequent ward, stowed out of con-
science
as unpopular luggage.
As I ride the subway
to spend half-an-hour with one, I revisage
who she was in the pomp and sumpture of her hey-
day,
when week-end visits were a presumptive joy,
not a good work. Am I cold to wish for a speedy
painless dormition, pray, as I know she prays,
that God or nature will abrupt her earthly function?"[66]

The poem that follows from Ronald Blythe's collection
called up for me so many memories of visiting older folk.
There is pathos, empathy, and most of all identification with
certain of these lines. I wonder which ones you think might
fit you one day?

Old: yet unchanged; still pottering in his thought;
Still eagerly enslaved by books and print;
Less plagued, perhaps, by rigid musts and oughts,
But no less frantic in vain argument;
Punctual at meals...
Rebellious, tractable, childish — long gone grey!
Impatient, volatile, tongue wearying not —
taught to pray.
"Childish" indeed! a waif on shingle shelf
Fronting the rippled sands, the sun, the sea;
And nought but his marooned precarious self
For questing consciousness and will to be:
Too frail a basket for so many eggs —
Loose-woven; gosling? Cygnet? Laugh or weep?
Or is the cup at richest in its dregs?
The actual realest on the verge of sleep?
A foolish, fond old man, his bed-time nigh,
Who still at western window stays to win

A transient respite from the latening sky,
And scarce can bear it when the sun goes in.
De la Mare[67]
Less drastic, perhaps we can identify more willingly
with this paragraph by Charles Lamb about a clerk who re-
tires at 50 after working since age 14, 10hrs/day, 6 days/
week.
"I am no longer clerk to the Firm of _____. I am Retired Leisure. I am to be met with in trim gardens. I am already come to be known by my vacant face and careless
gesture, perambulating at no fixed pace, nor with any settled
purpose. I walk about; not to and from."[68]
A prayer:
Oh my God, trapped in the truth seen by the literary
eye, I feel frightened, diminished. But you are greater
than the writer's pen, and it is in you I seek salvation,
not only from sin, but from the human condition itself. When sadness seems to overwhelm, let me turn
to your Words for hope.

FOR PERSONAL REFLECTION AND GROUP SHARING:
  1. What are your favorite passages from literature about
     aging; or from your own writing?
  2. What lines from the above chapter meant something
     special for you? Why?

Wisdom from Medical and Sociological Research

Coming from a philosophical background, I find medical
and sociological research hard to evaluate. Philosophers
prefer absolute truths concerning such matters as the meaning of life, unchanging truth, ethical absolutes, and proofs
for the existence of God. The results of medical studies or

observations about societies past and present seem at best highly probably and therefore kind of shaky to most philosophers. On the other hand, like everyone else in the universe, we are much impressed by facts coming from areas of research different from our own fields. Even if this data is not beyond reversal at some future time, it is significant, especially when it shows us a perspective we have not considered before.

Facts and Figures

Here are some "facts" about aging I found that caused me to think about it in a new way:

"85% of adults over the age of sixty-five years do not develop any form of dementia. Dementia is not a normal part of aging! ...benign forgetfulness, usually under pressure, is not progressive or disabling...Some reversible causes of dementia are nutritional and vitamin deficiencies, drug intoxication, thyroid and blood chemistry imbalances and tumors...making lists and reminder notes helps with forgetting."[69]

(Like many others, I tend to think that dementia is almost inevitable and to imagine that every time I forget something small or large it is a sign I am going downhill fast. If the above is truly a fact, then I should revise my thinking, shrug off lapses, and refuse to let fear discourage me.)

"85% of men die with a woman to take care of them; 85% of women die alone."[70]

(This statistic made me think that it is not an optical illusion that there are more single older women around than single older men.)

"Around 1900 the average age at death was 40, so it was an exception to go gray, reach menopause, retire, or become senile."[71]

(Maybe it's not an accident, in this case, that many of us feel we don't really know that much about how to age. Our grandparents died much earlier, probably, than we will. So we have only one generation to go by.)

(Part of a ten year MacArthur Foundation study) "Half of all the people in the history of mankind who lived to 65 are alive. And 70% of Americans live well beyond the traditional retirement age of 65...the main ways to age well are: stop smoking, eat right, exercise, watch your weight, control your blood pressure."[72]

(As we enter into the era sometimes called "the greying of America," by the year 2,000, 16% of the population will be 65 and older — we need more than ever to think about these later decades — how to make the most of them in terms of more healthy living and how to meet God at the time of life from retirement onward.)

"Three million people over sixty are alcoholics or have some kind of drinking problem...20% in hospitals have some drinking problem. 8% of hospital admissions of the elderly are for alcoholism. Alcohol effects the elderly body more intensely. Many fractures are increased by drinking because it decreases bone density...correlation between depression, suicide and alcoholism...Doctors in denial of their own drinking will not want to diagnose patients as alcoholic."[73] Social isolation is often related to late onset drinking.

(These statistics gave me pause to think about the importance of 12 step programs for the elderly. Slogans such as "Let go, let God," and "One day at a time," may turn out to have a special relevance for retired people as an antidote to escapism.)

Our Culture and Aging

In this section I plan to concentrate on ideas coming from two main sources: a series of tapes by Betty Friedan based on her book *The Fountain of Age*; and Ronald Blythe's *The View in Winter.*

Before summarizing and excerpting from these writers, there are a few ideas from other sources I found worth sharing with you:

Dr. Diane Piland, educator and pastoral counselor from Franciscan University of Steubenville, says that people should not wait until they age to become more spiritual. As you age your best traits tend to get better, but your worst traits such as hate, bitterness, and unforgiveness, also increase. Struggle against these bad traits early on, she recommends. A stubborn and belligerent demeanor puts off those who could help you. "You should have many years of bringing hurts to the Lord so that His sweetness can be seen in you."

Dr. Yvonne Rosedale, a professor who teaches geriatrics at Nazareth College of Rochester, N.Y., often advises: "Use it or lose it!" If you let yourself sink into inertia then you lose your skills, such as memory. In her course she quotes studies showing that keeping up mental capacities requires not just watching TV, reading and chatting, but also learning new skills, doing puzzles, playing games.

This quotation from an article in a newspaper raises a similar point: "Whistler's Mother was 67 years old and not ill. But she was acting the way she was supposed to act. Perhaps it symbolized the 19th century view of proper old age: sit quietly and wait for the end. It reminds us of how greatly the realities of aging and, more slowly, the perceptions of older people have changed during the past 100 years."[74] I had a mixed reaction to that one. There is a happy way that I feel "right," sitting in a chair, quietly knitting, vs. trying to keep up with younger goals. Still, I can see that if I gave up all my former career activities such as writing and teaching, I could become prematurely ancient.

A theme that runs through studies by many writers about aging is well expressed in this paragraph:

"I have learned that a culture which equates material possessions with success, and views the frantic, compulsive consumer as the perfect citizen, can afford little space for the aged human being. They are past competing, they are out of the game. We live in a culture which endorses what has been called "human obsolescence." After adolescence, obsolescence. To the junk heap, the nursing home, the retirement village, the "Last Resort."[75]

Gail Sheehy, author of the best-seller *Passages*, wrote a new book about men's passages. Some highlights about aging of men in an article by her for a popular magazine include these:

"Women feel pangs over losing their youth. Men feel dread."

"Men chase women because they're afraid of death."

" There is terror in a man of losing strength and control. For some it is greater than the fear of dying. Rationally, a man who is sick knows he must submit to being helped. But to contemplate helplessness and dependency, even temporarily, may resurrect fears of being a Mama's boy. The 'Action Man' just pushes harder, determined to 'punch through the pain' until he drops." He needs to accept his need for help. Otherwise he may die of heart trouble.

"Are you (men) willing to risk deeper intimacy that will offer you a buffer against the inevitable losses of middle and later life?"

"Traditionally, people have spent their young and middle adulthood working hard so that they can be comfortable in old age. But that's the last thing we want to be — too comfortable. We want to be active, engaged, useful...Men who live to 100 tend to be their own bosses and do not retire early."[76]

To turn now to ideas from longer presentations concerning problems of aging, I will start with Betty Friedan's taped rendition of her book *The Fountain of Age.*[77] The choice of this particular woman's research for inclusion in a book about aging in Christ may seem odd. After all, in Christian circles Friedan is best known as the radical feminist author of *The Feminine Mystique* and an open advocate of the choice of abortion for women. Actually it is somewhat of an accident that I listened to Friedan's vocal taped reading of her aging book. A friend who knew I was writing about the same subject handed it to me. I thought I would give it back after five minutes of listening. But, instead, I found myself thoroughly engrossed. So, I hope you, the reader of my book, will set aside your feelings about Betty Friedan, the activist, so you can take in the interesting facts and ideas she gathered together for *The Fountain of Age*.

Friedan's book begins with a personal admission. When she reached the age of sixty, this vital activist woman couldn't face the idea of being old. A seeker and a researcher, Friedan devoted much time to trying to see what aging meant in our culture and how to come to a more hopeful image of these years for herself and her readers.

(Note: since these ideas were taken off the tape, there are no footnote references with page numbers)

Studying the media in relation to aging, Friedan came up with some interesting facts:

Prime time TV showed only 1.5% of performers over 64 years of age.

Only 2% of TV commercials had older characters.

Of 265 articles on aging, none showed older people to be active but showed them all to be in nursing homes.

Out of 275 illustrations in Vogue magazine, only one might have been over sixty.

MS Magazine had no older women.

"Forever Young", a plastic surgery operation in 1984 claimed that 477,000 people used certified plastic surgeons, most of these being women over fifty.

In the media most images of the elderly are from nursing homes validating our thinking about aging as involving senility, incontinence, and incompetency.

Old women are talked about in films jokingly as hags, nags, and witches.

Stimulation leads to increase in brain capacity.

Women who combined child-raising with work outside the home have less difficulty with aging. This difference is largely due to the "empty nest" syndrome where women who have not worked in the world have a larger loss of identity when the children leave the home than women whose identity combined both roles.

Women are more used to changing roles than men and therefore deal better with aging. Women see aging as allowing them to have less concern with externals and more with their interior lives.

Men experience much depression between the ages of 64-70.

All elderly people need to shift from family, ego, and career goals to aspirations to wholeness and meaning.

Friedan thinks that retirement villages often involve denial of aging.

Only 15% of the population need the type of care offered by many elderly communities. Intimacy in community is more needed than care for most people. Age itself is not a disease! Doctors should have as their goal to improve the quality of life to the older person, not just to prevent or cure disease. Treatment of illness can sometimes lead to less quality of life than the disability would have entailed.

Many retired people do better in the cold climates they grew up in than in their warm, stagnant retirement colonies.

Friedan approves of a new arrangements for the elderly such as houses with separate bedrooms but a common kitchen.

It is good that there is now more training of older people in peer counseling, hospice, participation in social action.

Friedan ends her tape (book) on a note of liberation. We should be happy to be ourselves at this later time of life. With integrity and generativity we can move into the unknown future.

Throughout this book you have been reading excerpts from *The View in Winter* by Ronald Blythe. Actually there is a somewhat sentimental reason. My twin-sister, Carla De Sola, gave my mother this book in the last decade of her life. My mother evidently liked the book so much that it sat on her coffee table for years. The cover depicts two deck chairs facing a river. In one of them we see just the hat and legs of a seated man, presumably an old one. I imagine this often seen cover impressed itself into my mind in such a way that when I was digging around in an old closet for books about aging I regarded it as an old friend. In fact, it has turned out to be a treasure trove. The big surprise, after reading narrative after narrative in *The View in Winter* from a seemingly secular viewpoint only, was that in the last chapters the author's interviews become progressively Christian in content.

It's about time you know a little bit more about this sociologist Ronald Blythe who has been helping us understand aging for so many pages already.

Born in 1922, and educated in rural East Anglia, England, Blythe began writing in 1954. A local historian and a storyteller, his books include a collection of short stories, a novel, a study of Britain between the two world wars and *Akenfield*, the portrait of English rural life for which he is best known and widely acclaimed. He has also written critical introductions to the works of Jane Austen, Thomas Hardy and Leo Tolstoy. Blythe is a Fellow of the royal Society of Literature. At the time of publication of *The View in Winter*, Blythe was living and working in East Anglia in a sixteenth-century farmhouse by the Stour River.

Blythe wrote *The View in Winter — Reflections on Old Age* in 1979 because he realized that people were living longer and longer — something very new at that time. He interviewed hundreds of elderly (most of them over 75) in the 1970's to see how they were getting along, what ideas or advice they had on aging, why some of them were happy and/or active and others were not.

The introductory pages of the book present some of Blythe's own insights about the tensions and challenges the elderly face:

"The most irreconcilable aspect of age is the destruction of progressive movement, that hard fact of having come to the end of the journey when custom and instinct still insist that one can and should go on. And the major frustration is, I simply can't go on."[78]

I believe that these moments of "I can't go on," take place in stages. For me, first came I can't stay up late and I can't move with speed. Then, I can't travel around the world as a speaker — at least not at the former pace. Next, perhaps, will be I can't go out in the evening. With many other activities it is more a matter of just slowing down. A character interviewed by Blythe puts it this way, and the image has remained in my mind as a kind of comfort: "What you can't do in one day, you must do in two."

What would your list of things you can't do any more include?

"Old age is not an emancipation from desire. For most of us that is a large part of its tragedy. They want their professional status back, or their looks, or their circle (of friends), or sex."[79]

I find this observation to be poignantly true. But it is not a constant state of longing for the same old things. I can go for months not wanting to look younger, for instance. What do you miss the most from the past?

"Is it any wonder that, with so many contemporaries dead and so many signposts...obliterated, a lot of thought and energy goes into repeating who you are, both to the young and to yourself?"[80]

Sadness! I push forward my old Catholic truths upon my family who roll their eyes and groan; except, of course, when they are in real trouble. Then they beg me to pray for them — old-fashioned style, too! In what ways might you assert your separate identity as Blythe suggests?

Although, a few of the old people Blythe interviewed were happy to get rid of clutter, make new friends and welcome solitude; most still wanted what they had had, and most of all they wanted to be needed, wanted and loved. In that desire to be needed and loved lies a certain tension with the middle-aged and the young. As Blythe reports,

"The increasing demands and needs of the large number of people living into their 70's, 80's, and even 90's have produced helplessness, guilt and resentment in the younger relatives. Many are not ready for the role-reversal of having to care for their parents rather than vice-versa. Many old people reduce life to such trifling routines that they cause the rest of us to turn away in revulsion." He mentions not doing anything useful, but spending time just eating, playing bingo, consuming excessive amounts of drugs. One of the most dreadful sights is...long rows of (elderly) women playing the Las Vegas slot machines. Had Dante heard of it he would have cleared a space for it in Hell.

"A truth which can nowadays only be whispered about the old is that they can be boring, cruel or disgusting, and that they can make the middle-aged ill...the geriatric care (of their parents) is often so overwhelming that it begins to eat away at the respect and affection which the children have for their parents...It is not just a reluctance to take on a burden which causes this corrosion, but the emotional shock and resentment at the reversal of roles...Perhaps, with full-span lives the norm, people may need to learn how to be aged as they once had to learn to be adult."[81]

Sometimes we glamorize the past in this regard imagining that before our frenetic age of everyone working outside the home, old folks were taken care of beautifully by doting family members. This passage from an interview Blythe did with an elderly nurse, disabused me of that idea:

"(In the past, the elderly) had nothing to do all day, so they'd stare out the window. Today, they stare at the telly. In the 1920's they would be living with grown children, but totally neglected — 'dreadfully dirty.' They sat about and stank. And some of them were right tartars and families would long for them to die. But other old people were gentle and good. Full of prayer, I suppose."[82]

On a cheerier note, concerning retirement before total disability sets in, we have this delightful narrative by a farmer: "The only retirement feeling I have is one of relief. I feel that I can go off whenever and wherever I like and be independent. I like to be out, I like to be away! Away, away! Or just out gardening. Here, there and everywhere, that's me. I don't stay in, I get out. I'm always out. I like to be out. Being out keeps me free, so I'm out whenever I can. I feel I'll live if I'm out. I know you can have dreams which give you the impression that you are out of the body, but I've experienced this thing so vividly that I've had to acknowledge that, for a time, I really was outside."[83]

That farmer explained how one time he was in the war, though actually at home in workshop, and another, when he was actually in bed, but felt he was out in the field.

I myself experience much change of mood from even going from my lower level suite up to the main house where the children are frolicking about, or from taking a bath, or, even more, from walking outside, even just to go to the mailbox. I think the semi-retired have more time to notice changes of mood. What is your experience?

This observation of Blythe corresponds with what people tell me at aging workshops. See if you agree:

"The young do not want to be old, nor do they entirely believe that they ever could be, and the old, generally speaking, do not wish to be young. Once through the gamut of time is enough for most people. What usually occurs is that an aged man still finds life surprisingly sweet and desires more agedness, but not a full repeat trip."[84]

On older lady Blythe interviewed liked to sit in a park and watch children play because it helped her forget herself: "You get very sick of 'me' when you're my age. I daresay that that's the worst of being old, having all this 'me' in your head!"[85]

I was glad to read that passage. Perhaps it explained to me why I enjoy being a spectator so much more in my older years. Who or what do you like to watch as an escape from introspection?

Editing this manuscript, I suddenly thought, "Why am I putting these narratives under wisdom from sociological research? They are not expert opinions but just what folks might say." Then, I realized, happily, that this was Blythe's whole point — wisdom of the sociologist is coming from his warm, interested, contact with the people. It is their wisdom, not just his, that is the truth for all ages.

Again and again in all my readings, I came upon the question of attitude. The difference between a miserable and a good old age has so much to do with ones general view of life. Here are lines from a women of eighty-two:

"Life is so very sweet, isn't it? So very sweet, I think. I still find it sweet. If you make it miserable and dull, then it is you and not life that is to blame. I don't resent being old at all — except it would be nice to be forty again! I would then have so much life left to come. You know new things when you are old and you say to yourself, 'I wish I had this much brains when I was younger.' Wisdom, you know. You think a lot and see things in a different light. I see a light which is not what I saw back in the twenties.

...I've been living here for fifty-seven years. All my family has been born and brought up in this house, so it means more than a house, you might say.

...We'll eventually meet on the same train, won't we? We're all journeying to where God is, aren't we?"[86]

Others find that the loss of a life companion, in this case a roommate of the same sex, leads to a devastating change in outlook. Until it actually happened, Blythe reports, the highly educated woman he interviewed believed that self-control, common sense, and her Christianity would see her through this final phase. She knew it would be sad (when her friend died first) and she accepted its disruption, but nothing prepared her for the extent of her suffering and upset. Grief has become...too genuine and actual to be exorcized by therapy or drugs.

"I can't read very well and it was the reading which I liked most. I go on crying all the time. That is what I mostly do now, cry. I try to meet things. I think that is what one must do now. You can't say that 'I can't like this' or 'I won't like that.' When you are old you must meet a situation — there is no other alternative. I certainly feel very isolated — I do feel that. It is a strange thing, really. They've all passed away. All the real friends are gone. There are none left of the friends of my lifetime. The greatest friend was the last to go.

My day has quite gone. It is over. Quite gone. It is all very different now and difficult to understand. There is nothing I can do here, although everybody is kind. It is too steep to walk to the library and too hard to walk anywhere. I need to be somewhere where I can do more things. I certainly want to walk. There is a bus here, but I can't manage it. There are no cars to hire. The world belongs to the young.

As for old age, you are expected to accept it. You know you are a back number. I don't resent it. I don't expect what I expected when I was young. I don't even think of it. You take a simple thing such as whether somebody likes you are they don't. It doesn't cross your mind when you are very old. I don't expect to be liked or disliked. I don't expect *anything*. I don't expect anyone to do anything for me, but when they do I say, 'How kind they are,' and mean it.

...I treasure my brain-power. I hoard it. You really must have memories. They are all you have left, and if you didn't have them you would think about what is happening now, and it would be fatal...I have complete faith in that there is another life. So there is a greater experience soon."[87]

Let me end this excursion into the world of the English elderly as studied by Blythe with this quotation from an aging religious: "They say we are going downhill — but they are wrong. We are going *up*hill, which is why it is such heavy going!"[88]

A prayer:

All those voices about aging in our culture. Some sound like me. Some sound very different. Please, Lord of the Word, let me hear your voice when my mind becomes still. Let me not be so inured in my culture that I cannot come into yours. Or, rather, let my culture be simply your kingdom!

FOR PERSONAL REFLECTION AND GROUP SHARING:

1. How do you feel about the greater length of life in our times as compared to a century ago or even how it was when you were growing up?
2. Which of the facts given in this chapter were new to you? What statistics have you read which startled you?
3. Do you agree with some of the researchers in this chapter that society views the aging mostly in a negative manner?
4. Going through the chapter, what are the ideas you think wise or, on the contrary, seem contrived or limited in perspective?

Wisdom from Psychology

In an area as broad as healthy aging, there is a lot of overlap between psychology and the sociological perspectives of the previous section. Now it is time to share insights coming from experts who are professional psychologists with a special interest in the field of geriatrics. Again, there is not completeness. As soon as I began to investigate, I found the material to be so voluminous that it could never be summarized in a book of this scope. Instead, I am bringing you ideas from my random reading. I imagine that it will lead some readers to want to study further.

Before presenting ideas from whole books about psychology of aging, I want to include some shorter concepts I found helpful coming from magazine articles:

"Age is an identifying characteristic that allows others to locate us in time and history. Concealing our age only perpetuates the notion that there's something shameful about growing older."[89]

"Forget about trying to reverse the process. It's never been a better time to face up to aging. In fact, getting older truly does mean getting better. However, men and women are buying age-fighting weaponry."[90]

There excerpts interested me because I have always thought it was shameful to be ashamed of age. At thirty-five, in a spirit of bravado, I responded to birthday greetings with a jaunty: "I'm thirty-five, half-way to eternity!" On the other hand, I have come to understand that given the very real negative stereotypes in our society, it is understandable why many people just can't stand announcing the number of years they have lived at each birthday. There are still men over fifty who regard women over thirty-nine as over-the-hill. Some women in their thirties regard men over sixty as beyond the pale. In spite of laws about agism, there are employers who consider those of both sexes over sixty to be too old. Given all that, is it surprising that many try to conceal their ages?

In the issue of *Psychology Today* I have quoted from above, there are these remarks from aging expert Renee Garfinkel, Ph.D.:

"It's not simply that we tend to keep our health longer; it's that we also aren't subject to generational restrictions on behavior, career choices, or clothing...We can roller-blade, go back to college, wear jeans and sweaters, etc. at any age and not seem unusual."[91]

Surprisingly, Garfinkel claims that rates of depression tend to decline after the age of forty-five, for both men and women. (There's a slight — but temporary — blip in men's rates around the time of retirement.)

Other research about aging found in that issue of *Psychology Today* shows that our sense of what we deem most important for happiness tends to alter appropriately as we age, a sign of the true resilience of the human spirit: we may not look as fresh-faced, but we like ourselves more. We actually think fewer negative thoughts. Life becomes simpler. Men become more accommodating and emotionally expressive; women more assertive and active in meeting their own needs.

A twelve step slogan that fits the last sentence goes: "It's easier to wear slippers than to carpet the world." Part of being in the single state, by choice or circumstance, is that absence of spouses to meet needs such as doing the laundry, fixing things, helping buy a car, etc. I notice as a widow that though I have to grit my teeth to learn something new such as how to pump gas at the self-serve when there are no full-serve lanes left in a town, once I have mastered the new skill sufficiently to get along there is a certain sense of pride. It is certainly easier to learn how to insert the gas nozzle into the tank than to find a "perfect male" partner for the rest of my life! And I imagine the males referred to above who learn how to be more emotionally expressive also start out more from necessity than desire. Husbands no longer competing in the work-place and now spending most of their time at home with their wives can afford to let go of stoic stances that are no longer imperative for a successful masculine image in the outside world.

I liked the ideas that follow about working ones way through fear of aging from Dr. Wayne E. Oates, a professor of psychiatry and behavioral sciences who teaches psychology of religion and pastoral care:

"Keep on giving of yourself — and receive graciously. The world needs you! — your wisdom, foresight and compassion. Remain open and listen well to those around you.

"Make friends of all ages. Older friends can give you wisdom about coping with aging. Younger friends will renew your spirit for you and their visions will inspire you.

"Learn new skills. If you identify with one skill, and then outlive that skill, life might begin to seem over for you.

"Come to terms with losses you have sustained. Grieve fully, moving through the stages of shock, numbness, alternately accepting and rejecting the tragic reality, pouring out your sorrow in tears, and ultimately coming to a sense of peace with yourself and God.

"Envision a time when you are going to reorganize your life and get on with the challenges life has for you.

"Don't wallow in self-pity and despair. Assume that a certain amount of bad luck, suffering, disappointment, and grief are common to all. If you cannot pull yourself out of despair, consult your physician.

"Don't be afraid to ask for help

"Take inventory of factors that age you — smoking, poor diet, lack of exercise, over-exposure to sun, etc.

"Turn to God who is faithful throughout the years. Direct your energies to your interior, spiritual life."[92]

The part of this advice I found most important had to do with accepting losses. I think of the terrible grief of my husband and what I went through when our nineteen-year-old son committed suicide.[93] My husband died of cardiac arrest two years afterward. I don't think he went through all the stages of grief. Going even for a few months to grieving groups was a great help to me. Years later I sometimes see participants in these groups who seemed so devastated that they could never smile again, walking around in a joyful spirit. I am so grateful for the counselors who, often on a volunteer basis, staff such grieving groups.

I would now like to summarize insights I found in the book *Aging Successfully* by gerontologist George Lawton.[94] I have a personal reason for selecting this book for my research, even though it was written quite some time ago in 1946. When I was a pre-teen my mother got a job as an assistant to this very expert, George Lawton, to help him work on *Aging Successfully*. I only met Lawton once or twice, but I would hear tales every evening at supper about the book, and also about a TV program the psychologist hosted called "Life Begins at Eighty."

The published *Aging Successfully* sat proudly on my mother's own bookshelf when she was of the age they had been writing about, and eventually came to me after her death in her eighties. I paid no attention to it at all until arriving at the age of sixty and starting on my own book about aging. Naturally, I wanted to see what this pioneer gerontologist actually had to say about the subject that was now of such interest to me. I was not disappointed.

On the title page of *Aging Successfully*, I found this provocative quotation from the French writer Amiel: "How to grow old is the masterwork of wisdom, and one of the most difficult chapters in the great art of life."

Here is some of the wisdom I found in Lawton's book itself with some comments of my own in parentheses as I go along:

" Each adjustment (as I age) should be met realistically in terms of what is the problem and how can I deal with it. To succeed 10% is not zero percent."[95]

(Often I succeed in analyzing a problem of aging. Let's take adjusting to being marginalized in social situation where I would previously have been center-stage. I understand the problem, decide to resign myself to a more spectator role, and even resign myself to my new status in my mind. But then in four out of five situations where I cannot "shine," I feel, not resigned and content, but sad and depressed. Well, there we are, by Lawton's standard that would be succeeding 20% of the time. I should be glad of the one time of peaceful acceptance instead of grinding my teeth about the four times of failure.)

"We should seek long life to have time to do more things we have not done. Each period of life has its own beauty and usefulness..."[96]

"What makes someone old is losing interest in setting goals or in trying to achieve them."[97]

(When I first started on my semi-retirement, I was delighted. So much time to set personal goals instead of meeting deadlines or dealing with the pressures of speaking dates.

But pretty soon, in spite of lovely prayer times, interesting people to know, groups to lead or join, close family ties, and books to write at a leisurely pace, I found myself restless. Oftentimes a sense of inertia would overtake me regarding my activities. Finally, I was forced to realize that I need the structure of definite work situations to feel challenged. I have decided midway through writing this book to take up 2/3 time work in my teaching field again.)

"One could look at wrinkles and furrows not as defeat against aging but as badges and medals testifying to the wisdom and experience of life."[98]

"What we want to see in the face of an older woman are not the gorgeous tints and allure of twenty-five, but a rich, alive, inner security and satisfaction which is the fruit of experience."[99]

(It has always fascinated me how the face of someone we admire looks greatly beautiful even with wrinkles. Who would want to see photos of the youthful Mother Teresa only, or Gandhi as a teenager? And yet, we think of our own faces as ugly because of the wrinkles and lines and sagging flesh. It seems to me that when I am being exceptionally loving, my sense of inner beauty is sufficient and I don't care what the mirror tells. With this in mind, at lectures I used to tell groups of women, "When you look in the mirror, don't ask whether you look like Marilyn Monroe. Say instead to yourself — every day in every way, I look more like Mother Teresa!")

A concept Lawton developed at length that bears much introspective consideration is this one:

"Barrenness and unhappiness may have specific causes of longstanding in our way of life from before which we have to face. We need to risk change...to relinquish certain unjustified tyrannies...to develop a new point of view...I'm too old to change is not true but may become true because of the weight of emotional resistance."[100]

Lawton thinks that any problem we leave unsolved in our childhood will remain unsolved until the end. For example, a kid who was afraid of other kids and used sarcastic words to fight back, will probably also display too much vinegary wit in old age.

(A character problem I was only able to get help on in my late 50's was chronic irritability and outbursts of anger. I just assumed I would be suffering from this and making other people suffer, also, all my life. Happily, I ran into a fantastic self-help group called Recovery, Inc., (for anger, fear, depression) developed by a brilliant psychologist in the 1940's. After a few years in the group, even my family was amazed at the change. I still blow up when all my buttons are pushed, but not every day as before. For more information on these groups meeting all over the world, see footnote 13.)[101]

Here is an insight from Lawton especially good for men to ponder. The psychologists claim that many men have greater difficulty with aging because they have identified their worth with physical strength and earning money. This fits with the way retired men get satisfaction from running something like a lodge or a kiddie team.[102]

A related problem for older men is not having outlets for their manly authority. Their children are usually either challenging their authority or have left and turned their backs on it. Lawton thinks that as early as their forties, men have to start establishing their identity on another plane. Using some of his energies for a cause or creative expression means that the outlets will be there later after retirement. If causes and creativity are not natural interests, then men can always enjoy thinking and observing, learning and meditation.[103]

To be youthful in mind, Lawton constantly emphasizes, means to love new experiences, to judge each day on its own terms...to see life as unpredictable, to value oneself as a person rather than to think ones value has to do with what one possesses or whom one can impress.

(It is certainly my experience that men and women of high energy can become deflated when there is nobody to tell what to do. Sometimes, I think, constant giving of unwanted advice is a substitute for a previous role of authority. It seems that simple volunteer work, such as St. Vincent de Paul where the older person is constantly in contact with people who not only need but want advice, can be a wonderful way to overcome such a problem.)

Concerning loss of sexual prowess, Lawton devised a wonderful analogy:

"The man of sixty-five does not become an ascetic or celibate. He turns to other instruments in that symphony orchestra we call love. Sometimes he feels that nothing can compensate him for the loss of the physical. But passion tends to be a solo instrument that is likely to drown out all the other voices in the orchestra. As it grows weaker, the other instruments have a chance to be heard. The normal man and his wife wonder whether they may not have gained by the change. When the sun, one object of beauty, goes down, one can see the stars, other objects of beauty."[104]

Perhaps a man might identify with this observation of our gerontologist author.

Concerning retirement, Lawton talks about the shock of the farewell dinner full of accolades and then the mourning afterwards. "At the parting dinner, they covered me with garlands, then exiled me from the human race and sent me off into the wilderness."[105]

Some retirees are happy as can be, feeling totally relieved to get out of the pressure of the dog-eat-dog, sometimes "lie, cheat and steal" world of their previous work sites. But many retirees feel miserable. Lawton thinks that this happens especially to those who have not cultivated leisure beforehand. Women do better than men because they rarely (when he wrote) identify totally with their work. Women always live in their home, whereas most men are not used to living at home all day. Men who have always puttered around the house doing things will be happier.

The very word "retirement," can have a distressing ring. Lawton suggests that what the older person wants is not to leave the world but to participate in a new way. We need goals and accomplishment without the strain and the pressure of work for pay.

As a widow missing the company of her husband, this insight of Lawton explained a lot. It is important, he thought, for men and women to engage in joint social activities. As long as they live, men and women must feel that they are still men or women. A women needs to have a conversation with a man once a day.

(Seeing men in Church every day is good for me. What started as a sort of joke has become a tradition: one particular older, married man hugs all the widows when he sees them walking past each morning. I also have formed a strong bond with the son-in-law I live with. I consider it a great gift of God to have him close with his physical strength, intelligence, humor, and love to support me.)

A few of Lawton's ideas about family love for the elderly proved interesting. He thinks that late marriages are good because there are less illusions and there can be joy in companionship. Older love is more tender. On the other hand, many will avoid a late marriage out of fear of death or physical helplessness.[106]

Sometimes, when I was reading Lawton's book, I thought that he sounded too optimistic. What about some of the obvious negatives of the way older people relate to others? About half way through *Aging Successfully*, the psychologist does get into those tangled areas of manipulation, power plays, with helpful suggestions for improvement.

On older parents relating to adult children, Lawton claims that pressure comes from over-attachment of older parents to the adult child. Endless protection destroys freedom. About an older person trying to live vicariously through the child, Lawton's remedy is a separate, active life for the older person. All sorts of manipulation and power plays come in: using bad health for leverage, regarding in-laws as intruders, etc. Sometimes the adult children are overly attached to fathers or mothers. He recommends genuinely helping roles for all persons concerned. [107]

I was wandering if Lawton would ever get around to the questions of physical pain and fear of death. When he did, his observations were challenging. Suffering, he thought, can be educative and lead us to become warmer, simpler and more sympathetic, and appreciative of the good instead of making us bitter.[108]

"Suffering from illnesses is terrible, but there is a marked difference between people who become overwhelmed and constantly complain and others who do not even elude to their pains in conversation."[109]

One problem of aging, over-criticalness, Lawton discussed in a way that has a lot of relevance to spirituality:

"An old man's disagreeableness represents disappointment and anger at being unloved. Could he put his feelings into words, this is what he would say; 'I want you to love me, but you won't be able to, because I'm not worthy of your love or that of anyone else, and so I hate you and all the world.' If the old person can't get affection and attention by being just what he is, he will try to get it by force, just as he used tantrums in childhood, though he is quite unaware of the similarity in method."[110]

Few of us would want to identify with the above critical, older person. But we need to ask ourselves if others do find us to be overly ready to, as my mother-in-law used to say, give others "the needles."

Lastly, here are some pithy one-liners form Lawton I want to remember:

We need to make new friends so that when the old ones die we have new ones.

We need to accept challenges — otherwise we rust.

Do what you have always postponed.

If you try to play it safe, that is a kind of hibernation.

Life is a struggle with different struggles at different ages.

Fatigue can often come from emotional conflict or boredom.

Do not try to live in the past or you will starve to death.

Avoid listing woes. Use conversation to draw others out.

Design your house to fit your needs — handrails, rubber mats in the tub.

There is lots more wisdom in Lawton than I could include here. Perhaps you don't know, many seem unaware, you can get almost any book that has ever been in print from the public library's inter-library loan service. Ask at the reference desk. *Aging Successfully* could be a choice you will be glad you made.

Let me introduce you now to another psychologist, specializing in geriatrics, with quite a different background. Henri Nouwen, born in Holland, was ordained a priest in 1957. He is the author of over 30 books on spirituality. He did graduate work in psychology at the Catholic University of Nijmegen and the Program for Religion and Psychiatry at the Menninger Clinic in Topika, Kansas. He has taught courses in psychology, spirituality and pastoral theology at the University of Notre Dame, the Pastoral Institute in Amsterdam, Yale Divinity school and Harvard Divinity School. He has lived with the Trappists at Genesee Abbey, the poor in South America and the mentally disabled in France and Canada. From 1986 until his death in 1996 he was pastor of the l'Arch-Daybreak community in Toronto, Canada.

There are references in many of his books to his work with the elderly. The one I read to cull wisdom for my book is written with Walter J. Gaffney, and is entitled: *Aging, The Fulfillment of Life.*[111]

The first excerpt I am presenting doesn't say anything much different from what we have read so far, but there is a deepening because of the introduction of a philosophical consideration about the nature of being vs. doing and having.

"...old age as the last segregation. This seems a very appropriate expression in a civilization in which 'being' is, in fact, considered less important than 'doing' and 'having'. Our desire to acquire a job, to make a good career, to have a house, a car, money, stocks and bonds, good relations, and a certain amount of knowledge, has become so central in our motivation to live that he or she who no longer is able to relate to the world in those 'desirable' terms has become a stranger...

"Segregation (of the elderly) often takes place in very subtle forms. Children write polite letters to their grandparents, but they write only what they think their grandparents want to hear. Younger people visit older people but seldom make them part of their lives, since they do not want to hurt, upset or shock them. Arguments are prevented, the truth hidden, and much of human reality kept out of sight...But, in fact, their (the elderly) lives become less human, less full and less real because, consciously or unconsciously, they have been forced into the prison of a selective communication which prevents them from seeing, understanding, and interpreting their own world as it is..."[112]

(I wondered as I read this how anyone, including myself, can avoid having negative feelings about aging if we have been segregating the elderly in our minds for decades in the way Nouwen describes?)

"Desolation is the crippling experience of the shrinking circle of friends with the devastating awareness that the few years left to live will not allow you to widen the circle again. Desolation is the gnawing feeling of being left behind by those who have been close and dear to you during the many years of life. It is the knowledge of the heart saying that nobody else will be as close to you as the friend you have lost, because a friend is like wine: 'When it grows old, you drink it with pleasure.'(Sirach 9:10)

"You have only one life cycle to live and only a few really entered that cycle and became your travel companions, sharing the moments of ecstasy and despair, as well as the long days of routine living. When they leave you, you know you have to travel on alone. Even to the friendly people you will meet on your way, you will never be able to say, 'Do you remember?', because they were not there when you lived. Then life becomes like a series of reflections in a broken window."[113]

(Some of my older friends who have "lost" many more beloved ones than I have claim that they get comfort from a running dialogue with the ones on the other side of time. The deeper the bond, they say, the more they can feel these ones as present.)

I hope I will never feel the kind of desolation Nouwen describes in the next paragraph. I know some who do and I labor in prayer to experience God's love with such reality that this will never be my fate.

"The most destructive (factor), is self-rejection. This is

the inner ostracism by which the elderly not only feel they
are no longer welcome in the society of profit, or able to
keep their small circle of intimate friends together, but by
which they also feel stripped of their own feeling of self-
worth and no longer at home in their most inner life.
He who has lost his inner self can say with Ben Sirach in
the Old Testament:
"O death, your sentence is welcome
to a man in want, whose strength is failing,
to a man worn out with age, worried about everything,
disaffected and beyond endurance." (Sirach 41:3-3)
"There can hardly be a more alienating feeling than that
which believes, 'I am who I was.' In this way they lose their
inner freedom and have no room for a creative response to
their loneliness. They are doomed to sourness, bitterness,
and cynicism; their future can be nothing else than emptiness, darkness and hell...They have opened the innermost
room of their sanctuary and allowed the evil forces to take
possession of it. This is not just theoretical speculation.
There *are* old people for whom there is only darkness. In
that darkness no color can be seen, so sign can be discov-
ered, no one can be trusted. This darkness can be filled with
resentment, anger, jealousy, and, sometimes, violent rage.
There is a powerful theme in human history from the Dark
Ages to Shakespeare and from Shakespeare's *Macbeth* to
Polanski"s *Rosemary's Baby*, telling us that indeed old men
and women can become warlocks and witches — ugly, ill-
tempered creatures who cast a dangerous spell on people
and spread a contagious fear wherever they go."[114]
(Rereading this passage to prepare my book, I realized
that it manifests one of my deepest fears — that the darkness will overtake me. Without faith in God, perhaps that
would be my destiny.)
Antidote to such desolation is to understand aging differ-

ently and ourselves, personally, as aging people differently. Many beautiful, hopeful thoughts about aging by Nouwen, from a spiritual viewpoint, will be included in the chapters to follow. Here is a foretaste:

"...think of old Pope John (the 23rd) giving life to an old church, and of an old Mother Teresa offering hope to the sick and dying in India. We look at the last self-portrait of Rembrandt and discover a depth that was not there before. We marvel at the last works of Michelangelo and realize they are his best. We remember the strong face of the old Schweitzer, the piercing eyes of the elderly Einstein, and the mild face of Pope Pius X. We recognize the transparency of the farmer looking over his fields in which he has worked for many years, the deep understanding smile of the woman who saw her own children die long before she did, and the concentrated expression on the face of the old poet. We hear people talking about the old country, the olden days, and old friends, as if their pains and joys had composed a melody that is growing to a silent climax."[115]

Here is a passage from another book of Nouwen, *With Burning Hearts: A Meditation on the Eucharistic Life*. It touches on a topic we have not dwelt on sufficiently — the sorrows that come with the loss of a dearly beloved person:

"When you are feeling only your losses, then everything around you speaks of them...the trees, the flowers, the clouds, the hills and valleys, they will reflect your sadness. They all become mourners...the winds whisper her name, the branches, heavy with leaves, weep for her...but as you keep walking forward with someone at your side, opening your heart, the mysterious truth that your friend's death was not just the end but also a new beginning, not just the cruelty of fate, but the necessary way to freedom, not just an ugly and gruesome destruction, but a suffering leading to glory, then you gradually discern a new song sounding through creation, and going

home corresponds to the deepest desire of your heart."[116]
And so, with these images of Nouwen, strong, sometimes upsetting, sometimes full of quiet joy, we end our
chapter on wisdom from the professionals and move on to
the wisdom of the Church.

To close with a prayer:
Please, please, please, my Jesus, shine your light into
the darkness of my fears and into the hearts of those
whose aging is bitter. When our natural strength ebbs
low, how we need you, and know it, too.

FOR PERSONAL REFLECTION AND GROUP SHARING:
1. Do you tell your age or conceal it?
2. Have you been able to accept losses? If not, what are your
   obstacles to seeking help through groups? Personal
   therapy?
3. What are long-standing problems in your character you
   think you are "too old to change"? Should you consider
   looking into paths to change so that your last years will be
   more loving and fruitful?
4. Do people think that you are over-critical? What ways of
   thinking help you to overcome this habit?
5. Do you sometimes segregate those older than yourself,
   relegating them to almost non-persons?
6. Have you experienced the sort of desolation in aging
   Nouwen writes about? How have you been released from
   such darkness in the past? If you are presently going
   through some of the negative feelings Nouwen mentions,
   what means are you taking to seek liberation?

WISDOM FROM THE CHURCH

*"He will wipe away every tear from their eyes, and death shall
be no more,*
*neither shall there be mourning nor crying nor pain any more,
for the former*
things have passed away." (Revelations 21:04)

Turning from narratives about the experience of aging
and the wisdom of professionals to the wisdom of the
Church is incredibly consoling. Here the sufferings of aging
are balanced by infinite vistas of fulfillment and joy in eternity for those who choose God and His ways.

On the other hand, the lives and writings of those who
have chosen God totally, the saints, reveal sufferings of a
more inescapable kind than those most of us will have to endure. Read on and see for yourself.

My own experience as a fervent Catholic is, the older I get,
the more I yearn to see the face of God. I am sick of my own
thoughts and preoccupations and eager for God — not insights
about God, but just God. At the same time, however, the very
yearning for eternity is painful, as well as the doubts and fears
that "sound" louder, less muffled by the worldly doings that
filled the past. The image of the older Mary of Nazareth helps
me. In her time she would have been considered old simply
by outliving her first-born and only son who died, we believe, at thirty-three. What must have been her hope, what
her anticipation, what her soul-stretch? St. Thomas Aquinas
once wrote that "As sailors are guided by a star to the port,
so are Christians guided to Heaven by Mary."

This long, long chapter about wisdom from the Church on aging will be divided in this way: lamentation and hope expressed in Scripture; inspiration from Christian spiritual writers, the witness of aging saints; and, finally, "at the gates of eternity" — Church teaching, rites and prayers concerning dying and the after-life.

From Scripture — Lamentation and Hope

Looking up various topics concerning aspects of aging in Scripture, I was surprised to find more for hope than lamentation. Then, I realized that the sufferings are "concealed" in the exhortations to hope. Older people needed to be told to hope in the Lord because their plight was so pitiful. The young were commanded to help widows because there were so many.

As you read the Scriptures I have selected, put a star next to those that express feelings you have now or used to have.

Lamentation:
"You shall not afflict any widow or orphan. If you do afflict them, and they cry out to me, I will surely hear their cry; and my wrath will burn..." (Exodus 22:22-23)
"...an evil spirit...rushed upon Saul, and he raved within his house..."
(1 Samuel 18:8)
The whole story of Saul's paranoid jealousy of David has often been used as an archetype of how older men can feel about younger rivals.
"Has not man a hard service upon earth, and are not his days like the days of a hireling? Like a slave who longs for the shadow...so I am allotted months of emptiness; and nights of misery are apportioned to

me...When I lie down I say, 'When shall I arise?' But the night is long, and I am full of tossing till the dawn...My days are swifter than a weaver's shuttle, and come to their end without hope...my eye will never again see good...Therefore I will not restrain my mouth; I will speak in the anguish of my spirit; I will complain in the bitterness of my soul...I loathe my life; I would not live forever...What is man that thou dost test him every moment? How long wilt thou...let me alone till I swallow my spittle?" (Job 7:1-20)

"Do not cast me off in the time of old age; forsake me not when my strength is spent." (Psalm 71:09)

"So even to old age and gray hairs. O God, do not forsake me, 'till I proclaim thy might to all the generations to come." (Psalm 71:18)

This passage about the suffering servant is not specifically about aging, but any elderly person who is in pain will identify with it:

"There was in him no stately bearing to make us look at him, nor appearance that would attract us to him. He was spurned and avoided by men, a man of suffering, accustomed to infirmity. One of those from whom men hide their faces, spurned, and we held him in no esteem. Yet it was our infirmities that he bore, our sufferings that he endured." (Isaiah 53:2-4)

"We receive good things from God; and shall we not accept evil? (Job 2:9-10)

Hope:

"As for yourself, you shall go to your fathers in peace; you shall be buried in a good old age." (Genesis 15:15)

"Now Abraham and Sarah were old, advanced in age; it had ceased to be with Sarah after the manner of women. So Sarah laughed to herself, saying, 'After I have grown old, and my husband is old, shall I have pleasure?' The Lord said to Abraham, 'Why did Sarah laugh, and say 'Shall I indeed bear a child, now that I am old?' Is anything too hard for the Lord? At the appointed time I will return to you, in the spring, and Sarah shall have a son.' (Genesis 18:11-14)

"The Lord visited Sarah as he had said, and the Lord did to Sarah as he had promised. And Sarah conceived, and bore Abraham a son in his old age at the time of which God had spoken to him." (Genesis 21:1-2)

"He executes Justice for the fatherless and the widow..." (Dt. 10:18)

The whole story of the widow who feeds her "last" cake to Elijah in 1 Kings 17 is worth reviewing, as is the story of Old Tobit in the book of that name to be found in Catholic Bibles.

"The Lord tears down the house of the proud, but maintains the widows boundaries." (Proverbs 15: 25)

"The Lord watches over the sojourners, he upholds the widow and the fatherless, but the way of the wicked he brings to ruin." (Psalm 146: 09)

"He shall be to you a restorer of life and a nourisher of your old age..." (Ruth 4:15)

The passage to follow reminded me of Shakespeare's oft-quoted phrase "all is ripeness," perhaps an echo, as is so much of the bard's writing, of his own reading of the Bible.

"You shall come to your grave in ripe old age, as a shock of grain comes up to the threshing floor in its season." (Job 5:26)

"Wisdom is with the aged, and understanding in length of days." (Job 12:12)

"Even though I walk through the valley of the shadow of death, I fear no evil; for thou art with me; thy rod and thy staff, they comfort me." (Psalm 23:4)

"Father of the fatherless and protector of widows is God in his holy habitation." (Psalm 68:5)

"They (the righteous) still bring forth fruit in old age, they are ever full of sap and green." (Psalm 92:14)

"(Bless the Lord) who satisfies you with good as long as you live, so that your youth is renewed like the eagle's." (Psalm 103:5)

"A wise son hears his father's instruction..." (Proverbs 113:1)

"Grandchildren are the crown of the aged, and the glory of sons is their fathers." (Proverbs 17:06)

"The glory of young men is their strength, but the beauty of old men is their gray hair." (Proverbs 20:29)

"Train up a child in the way he should go, and when he is old he will not depart from it." (Proverbs 22:6)

"Hearken to your father who begot you, and do not despise your mother when she is old." (Proverbs 23:22)

"A wise man is mightier than a strong man, and a man of knowledge than he who has strength." (Proverbs 24:5)

"...a man's wisdom makes his face shine, and the hardness of his countenance is changed." (Ecclesiastes 8:1)

"...learn to do good, seek justice, correct oppression; defend the fatherless, plead for the widow." (Isaiah 1:17)

"He will swallow up death for ever, and the Lord God will wipe away tears from all faces..." (Isaiah 25: 08)

"He gives power to the faint, and to him who has no might he increases strength. Even youths shall faint and be weary, and young men shall fall exhausted; but they who wait for the Lord shall renew their strength, they shall mount up with wings like eagles, they shall run and not be weary, they shall walk and not faint." (Isaiah 40: 29-31)

"Hearken to me, O house of Jacob, all the remnant of the house of Israel, who have been borne by me from your birth, carried from the womb; even to your old age I am He, and to your gray hairs I will carry you. I have made, and I will bear; I will carry and will save." (Isaiah 46: 3-4)

"And it shall come to pass afterward, that I will pour out my spirit on all flesh; your sons and daughters shall prophesy, your old men shall dream dreams, and your young men shall see visions." (Joel 2:28)

"Thus says the Lord of hosts: Old men and old women shall again sit in the streets of Jerusalem, each with staff in hand for very age." (Zechariah 8:4)

"And he went about all Galilee, teaching in their synagogues and preaching the gospel of the kingdom and healing every disease and every infirmity among the people...and they brought him all the sick, those afflicted with various diseases and pains, demoniacs, epileptics, and paralytics, and he healed them." (Matthew 4: 23-24)

"And behold, your kinswoman Elizabeth in her old age has also conceived a son; and this is the sixth month with her who was called barren. For with God nothing will be impossible." (Luke 1:36-37)

"There was a man in Jerusalem whose name was Simeon. This man was righteous and devout, awaiting the consolation of Israel, and the Holy Spirit was upon him. It had been revealed to him by the Holy Spirit that he would not see death before he saw the Messiah of the Lord. Prompted by the Spirit he came to the Temple; and when the parents brought in the child Jesus to perform the custom of the law in regard to Him, he took Him into his arms and blessed God, saying: 'Now, Master, you can let your servant go in peace, according to your word, for my eyes have seen your salvation which You prepared for all the nations to see, a light for revelation to the Gentiles, and the glory of your people Israel." (Luke 2:25-32)

"There was also a certain prophetess, Anna by name, daughter of Phanuel of the tribe of Asher. She had seen many days, having lived seven years with her husband after her marriage and then as a widow until she was eighty-four. She was constantly in the temple, worshiping day and night in fasting and prayer. Coming on the scene at this moment, she gave thanks to God and talked about the child to all who looked forward to the deliverance of Jerusalem." (Luke 2:36-38)

"Jesus answered him, 'Truly, truly I say to you, unless one is born anew, he cannot see the kingdom of God.' Nicodemus said to him, 'How can a man be born when he is old? Can he enter a second time into his mother's womb and be born?' Jesus answered 'Truly, truly, I say to you, unless one is born of water and the Spirit, he cannot enter the kingdom of God.'" (John 3:3)

"Do not rebuke an older man but exhort him as you would a father; treat younger men like brothers, older women like mothers, younger women like sisters, in all purity." (1 Timothy 5:1-2)

"Bid the older men be temperate, serious, sensible, sound in faith, in love, and in steadfastness. Bid the older women likewise to be reverent in behavior, not to be slanderers or slaves to drink; they are to teach what is good, and so train the young women to love their husbands and children, to be sensible, chaste, domestic, kind and submissive to their husbands, that the word of God may not be discredited." (Titus 2:2-8)

"So I exhort the elders among you, as a fellow elder and a witness of the sufferings of Christ as well as a partaker in the glory that is to be revealed. Tend the flock of God that is your charge, not by constraint but willingly, not for shameful gain but eagerly, not as domineering over those in your charge but being examples to the flock. And when the chief Shepherd is manifested you will obtain the unfading crown of glory. Likewise you that are younger be subject to the elders. Clothe yourselves, all of you, with humility toward one another, for 'God opposes the proud, but gives grace to the humble.'" (1 Peter 5:1-5)

"...he will wipe away every tear from their eyes, and death shall be no more, neither shall there be mourning nor crying nor pain any more, for the former things have passed away." (Rev. 21:04)

Any favorite Scriptures on aging I missed?

Inspiration from Christian Spirituality

Certain writers of full-length books provided me with invaluable insights about aging. Before telling you about these longer treatments, though, I would like to get you started by means of shorter passages that jumped out at me as helpful. In the questions for personal reflection and group sharing I will ask you if any of these quotations had an impact on you, so, if you are making use of those questions, you might choose to mark any of these passages you want to ponder.

The first such reading is from the fathers of the Church — a letter to the Romans by St. Ignatius, bishop and martyr:

"I am God's wheat and shall be ground by the teeth of wild animals.

I am writing to all the churches to let it be known that I will gladly die for God if only you do not stand in my way. I plead with you: show me no untimely kindness. Let me be food for the wild beasts, for they are my way to God. I am God's wheat and shall be ground by their teeth so that I may become Christ's pure bread. Pray to Christ for me that the animals will be the means of making me a sacrificial victim for God.

No earthly pleasures, no kingdoms of this world can benefit me in any way. I prefer death in Christ Jesus to power over the farthest limits of the earth. He who died in place of us is the one object of my quest. He who rose for our sakes is my one desire. The time for my birth is close at hand. Forgive me, my brothers. Do not stand in the way of my birth to real life; do not wish me stillborn. My desire is to belong to God. Do not, then, hand me back to the world. Do not try to tempt me with material things. Let me attain pure light. Only on my arrival there can I be fully a human being. Give me the privilege of imitating the passion of my God. If you have him in your heart, you will understand what I wish. You will sympathize with me because you will know what urges me on.

The prince of this world is determined to lay hold of me and to undermine my will which is intent on God. Let none of you here help him; instead show yourselves on my side, which is also God's side. Do not talk about Jesus Christ as long as you love this world. Do not harbor envious thoughts. And supposing I should see you, if then I should beg you to intervene on my behalf, do not believe what I say. Believe instead what I am now writing to you. For though I am alive as I write to you, still my real desire is to die. My love of this life has been crucified, and there is no yearning in me for any earthly thing. Rather within me is the living water which says deep inside me: 'Come to the Father.' I no longer take pleasure in perishable food or in the delights of this world. I want only God's bread, which is the flesh of Jesus Christ, formed of the seed of David, and for drink I crave his blood, which is love that cannot perish.

I am no longer willing to live a merely human life, and you can bring about my wish if you will. Please, then, do me this favor, so that you in turn may meet with equal kindness. Put briefly, this is my request: believe what I am saying to you. Jesus Christ himself will make it clear to you that I am saying the truth. Only truth can come from that mouth by which the Father has truly spoken. Pray for me that I may obtain my desire. I have not written to you as a mere man would, but as one who knows the mind of God. If I am condemned to suffer, I will take it that you wish me well. If my case is postponed, I can only think that you wish me harm."

(I quoted from this letter first because I believe that fear is one of the banes of old age. If we had the kind of detachment of St. Ignatius of Antioch we might even exult in our crosses, perhaps seeing our illnesses as the wild beasts that will devour us.)

St. Seraphim, the Russian holy man said "My body is in a state of decay, but my soul is like a new born babe."

(What a cheerful thought! The more I considered St. Seraphim's words, the more they sounded right. Why not think of my body as like a molting snake skin? Then I wouldn't mind so much watching and feeling it crumble.)

Along these lines, St. John Chysostom wrote:

"There is only one thing to be feared...only one trial and that is sin. I have told you this over and over again. All the rest is beside the point, whether you talk of plots, feuds, betrayals, slanders, abuses, confiscation of property, exile, swords, open sea or universal war. Whatever they may be, they are all fugitive and perishable. They touch the mortal body but wreak no harm on the watchful soul."[117]

How many of us could second the motion on this ironic statement of the great St. Augustine: "When men wish for old age for themselves, what else do they wish for but lengthened infirmity?"[118]

If any of you have ever come upon the extraordinary, mystical, medieval, wife and mother Margery Kempe, you would never be able to forget her. Here are some narratives about her aging days.[119]

In old age, Margery made a trip from England to Germany which included a pilgrimage to a sight where the host dripped with the precious blood. In those days of war, looting and rape, it was dangerous for a woman to travel alone. She paid a man to make part of the pilgrimage with her, but he was a strong, younger man and wanted to go faster than she could. He would keep going on ahead, not wanting her to slow him down. As she put in her journal, "He didn't care what became of me." It was something of a miracle that a lame woman about sixty years old should have kept up for days with a man who so wanted to get rid of her. She did get to her destination and was able to marvel at the miracle of the altar she had traveled to see.[120]

My favorite passage from the book concerns Margery's fear of death. To console her, Jesus tells her not to fear to die because He Himself will come and take her soul out of her body.

St. Ignatius of Loyola, the 16th century saint, lived himself for some 65 years. As you know, he founded the Society
of Jesus and also schools and missions all over the world.
St. Ignatius ended his life in Rome with alternating periods
of health and debilitating, painful illness.

In 1539, when he was about 50 years old, old for that
time, he wrote this letter to his sister-in-law after the death
of his brother, her husband:

"Upon learning of the good pleasure of God our Lord has
fulfilled by removing from these present sufferings the companion he gave you for a certain time in this life, I immediately did the best thing I could do for any person: I said
Mass for his soul at an altar where every time Mass is celebrated a soul is delivered from purgatory...we should not
weep while He rejoices or grieve while He is glad...Instead
we should look to ourselves — for we will come to the same
point as he — and live in such a way during this life that we
may live forever in the other."[121]

In a letter to someone whose sister died, Ignatius wrote:

"Having learned that God's will has been fulfilled in
withdrawing from the present trials of this life your sister...I
have many grounds and indications to assure me that she is
now in the other life, full of glory forever and ever. From
there, just as we remember her in our poor and unworthy
prayers, I am confident she will favor and repay us with
holy interest. And so if I were to go on at length with words
of consolation I would feel I was insulting you, since I am
sure that you conform yourself as you ought to the perfect
and everlasting providence which solely looks to your
greater glory."[122]

Of course, when someone we love and depend on dies, it
is only human to be cast down with grief. I don't believe
that Christ wants us only to rejoice at the thought that a pious loved one is now with Him. However, the thoughts of
the saints are an antidote to a kind of gray depression that

can often set in during the grieving process. We need to be confirmed in the faith that there is life after death, and a glorious one for those who are already united to Jesus on this earth by following Him and repenting for sin.

In a more literary style, we have this masterpiece of exhortation from the English martyr Blessed Robert Southwell:

"Ah fear, abortive imp of drooping mind; self-overthrow, false friend, root of remorse...ague of valor...love's frost, the mind of lies."[123]

And, in the same vein, we have St. Thomas More:

"I will not mistrust [God], though I shall feel myself weakening and on the verge of being overcome with fear...I trust he shall place his holy hand on me and in the stormy seas hold me up from drowning."[124]

To turn to another aspect of aging, flexibility in the seeking of new goals, I was delighted to find this quotation from a woman, St. Madeleine Sophie Barat:

"It shows weakness of mind to hold too much to the beaten track through fear of innovations. Times change and to keep up with them, we must modify our methods."[125]

Another holy woman, Blessed Raphaela Maria, wrote:

"Take shelter under our Lady's mantle, and do not fear. She will give you all you need. She is very rich, and besides is very generous with her children. She loves giving."[126]

All lovely thoughts, but what about all the negative sludge that clogs our minds between prayer and Mass times? Just as I was asking myself that question, I came upon this realistic quotation from a 20th century saint:

"Love Our Lady. And she will obtain abundant grace for you to help you conquer in your daily struggle, and the enemy will gain nothing by those foul things that continually seem to boil and rise within you, seeking to swallow up in their perfumed corruption the high ideals, the sublime determination that Christ Himself has set in your heart." (Venerable Jose Escriva)[127]

Before ending my section of smaller excerpts relevant to aging in Christ, I want to include a profound idea that was new to me. It came from a talk about the theology of a contemporary French philosopher, Fr. Marie Dominique. His concept of hope is that it is really a form of poverty. As we age, we become poorer, more dependent on God. This priest sees aging as a school for heaven where we will totally depend on God. As our natural powers diminish, we need more supernatural power, just to get from moment to moment.

Listening to this theory, I asked myself, if I slow down will I be able to enjoy the sustaining presence of Christ the more?

It is now time to turn to the work of some spiritual thinkers who have devoted themselves specifically to the question of aging in a spiritual way. The first author I want to acquaint you with, Richard Johnson, Ph.D., is a Christian counselor who gives workshops on spirituality of aging. He summarized his findings in a series called "Growing Older Gracefully: The Endless Horizon of God's Love," serialized in Liguorian Magazine in 1992.[128][129]

Here is the provocative beginning of Dr. Johnson's series:

"When viewed through human eyes alone, aging is nothing more than a succession of losses ending in nothingness, a painful descent into oblivion, and a senseless slippage of strength, stature, sensitivity and security, leading nowhere.

"As Christians, we are called to see beyond...Aging challenges us to remember that the Holy Spirit uses our natural human condition as a teaching aid so we can learn ever more personally the power of love...(and) our true reality as children of God...To teach us we are in the world but not of the world. Our journey is to Him (as our strength is taken away) a gentle reminder that we are headed toward a new life."[130]

Here are some more interesting viewpoints:
"We cannot grow from one stage to another without loss.
It is loss not gain, that produces growth. Aging is growth in
understanding peace and wisdom. We are to learn the virtues of acceptance, peace, faith, harmony, trust,
humility...As we grow in each new stage of life, we must
leave behind the previous one; if we hang on to the last, we
cannot move onto the next.

"Aging is hastened by fear. Love...is the wellspring of
vigor, the headwaters of freshness, and the waterfall of a
youthful spirit. Since God, who is love, is everywhere, love,
too, is everywhere.

"God tells us to fear not. The world fears aging because
it sees no achievement, only loss. As we continue to see our
aging as a product of God's love, we will increasingly become more youthful in spirit. Go from pessimism to gratitude, darkness to light, criticism to care.

"Take mini-vacations each day to meditate on the good.
May Sarton, after a mastectomy, said that the more our bodies fail us, the more naked and demanding is the spirit, the
more open and loving we can become if we are not afraid of
what we are and what we feel."[131]

Some of the insights in the above paragraphs could seem
too optimistic to some. If you find yourself reluctant to listen to this cheerful voice, read more slowly and consider
carefully — isn't it true that we are more loving even in the
midst of physical pain if we choose to trust in God? And
when we choose to sink under the burdens of life, don't we
find ourselves less and less able to love, instead coiled up in
our own misery?

In a later part of the series, Johnson goes more into our
need for relationship as we age. Concretely, we need to have
at least one person to share our personal concerns, to be understanding and appreciative, affirming. The self giving that
comes with volunteering is important in terms of interaction.[132]

I found the following observation somewhat startling. The truth of it managed to penetrate my defenses, since I am a person who greatly tends to the foible Johnson is pinpointing here:

"Live this moment well. Living in the past or the future robs us of vitality. 'If only,' 'I wish' leads to guilt and anger and fear. 'I should,' (has too much judging in it.)"[133]

There is a joyful way to relate to the past and future, of course, when we are grateful and hopeful. The negative way is to harbor grudges. This leads to fear for we are seeing only the dark side of others. "Each moment should be a link in the chain of loving forgiveness."[134]

Johnson insists that we not grant others the right to give us ulcers.

"Forgiveness does not mean we excuse the offender from responsibility. Forgiveness means ceasing to feel we have to claim recompense. Forgiveness means blessing the offender...we forgive not to let the other guy 'off the hook' but to bring peace into our own lives."[135]

Perhaps this sounds too facile. In the case of really bitter grievances perhaps you doubt if you can do it. Dr. Johnson, from long experience, suggests as an incentive to keep trying that: "We accelerate aging through anger rooted in fear. Fear keeps us tense. We must forgive unconditionally, not based on what the other does."[136]

Who wants to accelerate aging? I certainly can feel it in my body when I am stressed because of unresolved relationship problems. Johnson recommends substituting thoughtful understanding for speediness. Why should it be more important to accomplish tasks than to resolve disputes?

Another insightful comment of Johnson concerns finding new ways to be giving to others. He claims that lacking such loving roles can lead, instead, to adopting a mentality of entitlement. At first I wasn't sure what he meant. Then, examples came to mind. When my life is relatively empty and boring I keep wanting others to make it better. I feel "entitled," to more of their time. But when I am immersed in worthwhile activities, I am content just to be involved.[137]

Now we come to a point that, for me, turned out to be the concept of Johnson most helpful of anything I had come up with in my researches. It concerns the purpose of life during the aging stage. In the October '92 series segment, Johnson claims the purpose of aging is not more productivity, but instead, development in virtue. He is convinced that the reason God is giving us the later years is to become holy. If we stop wishing we could be more useful in the old sense, we may, indeed, develop to a greater degree the loving characteristics we have always longed to manifest. If we ask how aging can be part of God's loving plan when it has robbed us of our energy, Johnson urges us instead to see that our real work in life is not to produce, produce, produce, but simply to find God and live in His spirit.

Concretely, I translate this to mean that every day when I examine what happened, I should be measuring the day not in terms of how much I accomplished, but, rather, how loving I was to God and neighbor, period!

Johnson summarizes the benefits of his approach in this way:

"As hope advances so does peace. As humor enriches the soul, humility, transcending and kindness grow as well. As our growth in virtue progresses, our sense of life, love and joy moves in the same direction. The challenge of aging is to clearly recognize the many areas of personal and spiritual growth that present themselves daily as we mature."[138]

A few last pointers from Johnson:

"We need to relinquish the illusion we can control our own aging."[139]

"We do not have to allow our feelings full sway. We can decide which ones to allow to linger. (Steps include:) Identify the feeling; decide whether the thoughts that engender the feeling are rational; ask how Christ would want me to think and feel."[140]

"Jesus tells us to trust rather than to live in fear (Mk 6:50, Luke 12:32). When we resist aging as the world tells us, we feel fear. If we embrace it we experience joy, awe, and emotional richness."[141]

I loved these lines toward the end of Johnson's series: "Positive spiritual aging, maturing in God's love, stimulates feelings of wonder that lie too deep even for words. What we feel is the presence of God within us, a profound peace and awesome tranquility that brings us to the very edge of the lawns that surround our celestial goal. As our days pass we are called to grow ever more skillful in choosing feelings of love, more artistic in finding faith, and more heroic in harboring hope."[142]

Finally, Johnson advises us to close our eyes to the worldly light and look within, cleansed of illusions replaced by the reality of the Father's love.

Reading the excerpts from the Christian wisdom of Dr. Johnson, perhaps some of you felt, as I did, a kind of resistance. We may have become so used to fearing, doubting, and even despairing thoughts about aging, that so much positive input seems too good to be true. If you feel this way, don't give up. Read on. The effect of the wisdom of the Church is cumulative.

I now turn to quite a different spiritual writer; less psychological, more mystical — my dear friend and mentor, Charles Rich. This man who became a Catholic at thirty-three, coming from a Chasidic Jewish background in Hungary, died at 99 last year. A lay contemplative, who spent most of his day and night in prayer, Charles Rich, left a legacy of wonderful reflections about the spiritual life. One of the main themes of his writing was the yearning for eternity characteristic of holy souls throughout their lives, but on the increase as they age. In our section called "At the Gates of Eternity", I will share passages from his works about the transition from death to the fullness of life with Christ in heaven. The excerpts I am presenting now are more to wet your appetite and help you realize how enhanced your interior life could be if sentiments such as those of Charles Rich were yours, not just occasionally, but all day long. The following quotations are from a collection of his thoughts called *Reflections*.[143]

"This life is a journey...Some people mistakenly don't want to move on, and so they look upon old age as a kind of burden...We cannot stay forever in a world like this, and so it's good to be on the lookout for the day on which we shall have to depart from this life and exchange it for one that's infinitely more beautiful...As we grow older we begin to feel ourselves carried away from ourselves; old age makes us conscious of that part of our makeup that will live forever, and it weakens our hold on what has to pass away with time.

"...The years bring with them a wisdom that those who are young cannot possess, for youth oftentimes means perturbation and restlessness.

"The further away from holiness we are, the more perplexed we become, and it's this which makes old age such an unpleasant subject for some people to contemplate...It takes grace to love growing old.

"Youth is too passionate and unrestrained to love God purely, and so we can do this in a much better way when we receive the wisdom the years alone can bring with them."[144]

"Too many...fail to realize that everything they have and are is due to God's goodness and that without that goodness they would not even exist. Our sanctification lies in thanking God all the time...We cannot be happy unless we are saints, and we cannot be saints unless we think of Christ all the time."[145]

"It's the yearning for heaven that makes saints, and that yearning alone. The saints are not merely good people who perform acts of virtue."[146]

"The important thing is to yield up our whole being to God. Do we live for the things of the next life or the ones to be had in time? It is by means of such thoughts that we can find out whether we pray well...We can pray all the time and in all circumstances, there not being a minute in our life in which we cannot be given over to the admiration of all of God's works and become absorbed in the wonder of them. We can pray all the time by loving God in everything He has made, ourselves included. Without prayer nothing worthwhile can be achieved in this life, at least as far as the things of heaven are concerned. It is by prayer that the door to heaven is opened."[147]

"It's the personal experience of the divine that can fill up that void in our makeup which cannot be understood by our mind...God is not known to the extent He should be and that's why men are so unhappy in this life. They fail to find a motive for living, and so their life has no meaning...Unless we are carried away by the love for things eternal, we will find ourselves completely absorbed by what is of a nature to pass away with time."[148]

My friend, Judy Beshaw, who was selecting these excerpts for me, added in here that being absorbed by what is of a nature to pass away with time equals being lonely. I agree.

"The saints thought of eternity all the time. They couldn't get the thought of it out of their hearts and minds...Our salvation lies in thinking of Jesus, and, in so doing, with all we are. Heaven, with the happiness that's there, is close by because He who is Lord thereof is always present in our hearts and minds. Christ, the infinite bliss He is, is always around. He is closer to us than we are to ourselves."[149]

"It is not downward, to what is low in ourselves, that we have to fix the gaze of our soul, but to what lies beyond the reach of our mortal limits."

"Physically the saints lived in time, but spiritually in that somewhere else for which no name can be found...They prayed all the time because their love for things divine never knew any cessation...Living in uninterrupted communion with the divine, the saints took a completely different attitude towards all things that occurred in time, looking upon them all from a purely supernatural point of view, seeing and detecting God's designs in them...Everyone loves a saint because we detect in him what is not found in those who are not so dear to God.

"Man is so made that he must have an object in which to delight himself, and without such an object he cannot live. To most people, that object is something created by God such as friends, a sweetheart, father, mother, and so forth. To the saints, this object of delight is none other than He from whom all delight proceeds and whom the prophet designates 'the desired of all the nations' (Haggai 2:7) indicating in these words who and what our delight should be."

To close this segment with a prayer:

Dear Lord, all our lives we have been busy with many people and projects. Now, by means of the insights in this section, we feel ourselves being called to absorption in what is more central — the life of pure love of others and of you. Help us not to drift back into the periphery of daily life affairs. Let us do what is necessary in the world, but always be reaching out to the heavenly home you have made for us.

FOR PERSONAL REFLECTION AND GROUP SHARING:
What passages from the writers in this section of the book stood out for you? Why?

From the Witness of the Saints about Aging

The great love I have for the saints, leading me to write many books about them, comes originally from Charles Rich. The first time I met him in New York City, a few months after becoming a Catholic, he gazed at me with his fiery, mystical eyes and asked: "Do you want to be a saint?" I muttered something vague, not really having thought this possible even. "I hope you do, because I don't bother to make friends with anyone who doesn't want to be a saint. It would be too disappointing not to be with you in eternity!"

For that reason, it seems appropriate to begin my narratives about saints and aging with a few more quotations from Charles Rich:

"Sanctity is obtained by asking questions to which we will receive an answer after this life is over."[150]

"All throughout the sacred Scriptures we have been assured of the deep, incomprehensible love God has for us. With this in view, how can we have any misgivings as to the final outcome of our lives? It is due to God's goodness that we were born; it is due to His goodness that we shall die and continue on existing after this life is over.

"Would God have gone to the trouble of suffering and dying for us for the sake of a few years of our earthly life? He had our eternity in view when He made us out of nothing...no one can harm us except our own selves. The saints were not afraid of suffering and death. They knew it was by such means that they would go to heaven...If we truly love God we don't have to be afraid of anything, since He has a way of converting everything that happens for the greater good of our spiritual well-being."[151]

The pages that follow provide a witness of some of the saints who lived to an old age according to the standards of their times. Again, the selection is somewhat random. I think what I found will be sufficient, because you can always add information about other saints from your own storehouse of saints' books. As you read, mark passages you want to remember.

The Witness of St. Augustine

St. Augustine of Hippo was born in the year 354. In the year 426 at the age of seventy-two, he assembled his clergy and a large congregation and announced that he was retiring from the many duties of bishop though retaining the position and appointing his eventual successor.[152] At all other times of life, one looks forward to a future stage, "but an old man has no further state of life before him." His successor said, "The cricket chirps, the swan is silent."[153]

Augustine described himself at that time as a long-winded old man in ill health. To the end, he rejected costly gifts as unsuitable for a poor man. He claimed that expensive clothing "would look strange on these old limbs with my white hairs." Even though Augustine could not heal himself, he went about laying hands on the sick and wrote letters necessary in his diplomatic role for the sake of protecting his people from violent enemies. He also wrote diatribes to unworthy military leaders. Duties he still performed after his retirement included working out criteria for examining purported miracles involving relics.[154] Whereas in his early days he thought contemplation much more important than miracles; in his old age, Augustine thought that miraculous physical manifestations were necessary. People need some comfort when suffering from the incredible miseries life brings. Miracles hint at the resurrection of the body, especially those involving relics of martyrs.[155]

From the vantage point of 2,000 years of Christianity, it is hard for us to realize how discouraging the picture looked to Augustine at the beginning of the 5th century with Vandals coming right to his door in Egypt overthrowing Roman rule and torturing and killing the Christians en route. Our saintly bishop urged the other bishops to stay with their flocks instead of fleeing to safety. He lived to see whole cities sacked, virgins and ascetics scattered, and the Church buildings destroyed. It was hard to believe the gates of hell would not prevail over the Church.

The last years of his life, Augustine spent in his library editing his own writings, taking joy in the knowledge that they had helped people to love God. Augustine's last sermons are about love of life in relation to death. "If you love life so much as to want to have it, even after being fleeced by the enemy to become poor, think of how much you will love life eternal. All show by their love of life how much they desire to rise again after death."[156]

Augustine died in the year 430 urging his people to do penance for their worldliness, their boasting, and their anxiety about empty things. He asked that hangings with the penitential Psalms written on them be draped on the walls near his bed. Reading them and weeping for his sins, he asked to remain in solitude to pray for his friends, except at meal times.[157]

How human are those last four words!

The Witness of St. Francis of Assisi

Because of the famous movie, "Brother Sun and Sister Moon", most people picture St. Francis of Assisi only as a youth. In reality, he lived to what in his time was the ripe old age of forty-five. Information for this book comes from Jorgensen's biography of the saint.[158]

From 1223 till his death, Francis mainly lived as a hermit. Jorgensen wrote about this time in the saint's life that the health of the saint which had never been good, now got much worse:

"We see him in his youth attacked by one fever after another. Since then, his many and long fasts had undermined his constitution. Demons could drive him to the border of despair by saying to him, 'There is salvation for every sinner, except for him who has ruined himself by excessive penances!' He seldom ate food that was prepared, and dusted it in such case by throwing ashes on it, saying, that 'Sister ashes was chaste.' He slept but little, and then by choice sitting, or with a stone or log of wood for a pillow...he had hemorrhages form the stomach and the Brothers often believed his end was near." He (Francis) contracted the Egyptian eye sickness while in the Orient and often was nearly blind. He signed himself *homo caducus*, "a decrepit man."[159]

"In this last epoch of his life Francis sent out five letters...the themes of his writings were to serve and love God, to live a life of conversion, to fast — also in metaphorical sense to fast from sin and crime — to love and help our enemies, not to seek worldly wisdom or exalted positions, to pray much, to confess and approach the altar, to try to do good where we have been doing evil."[160]

In one letter, Francis described how a sinner dies:

"The body sickens, death approaches. The relatives and friends come and say, 'Prepare thy house!' And his wife and children, his nearest ones and his friends, act as if they wept. And the sick one looks around and sees them weep and is moved by a false emotion and thinks to himself, 'Yes, I will give over myself with soul and body and all that I have into your faithful hands!' Truly the man is damned, who gives his soul, his body and all he has, into such hands and depends upon them! Therefore the Lord says through the prophet, 'Cursed is he who depends upon a man!' And at once the priest is brought. And the priest says to him, 'Dost thou wish to do penance for all thy transgressions? The sick man answers, 'Yes.' And the priest asks, "Wilt thou give reparation to all whom thou hast defrauded and betrayed, as far as thou canst?' He answers, 'No.' And the priest says, 'Why not?' He answers, 'Because I have given all to my family and to my friends.' And thereby he misses his goal."[161]

Jorgensen comments that it is no comfortable picture Francis sketched, of these selfish "nearest ones" who stand around the bed of the dying man, and willingly let him go to hell, as long as they can get him to make a will in their favor.

Other themes in these final letters were great reverence for the sacrament of the altar, praying the Office with inner devotion, not just melody of voice, keeping altar cloths and vessels "shiningly clean" and living like the poor.[162]

"'No one,' said he, 'ought to consider himself a true servant of God who is not tried by many temptations and trials. Temptations overcome are a sort of betrothal ring God gives the soul.' He wrote that the perfect friar must embrace poverty, be simple and pure, chaste, intelligent and eloquent, have his mind fixed on God, always praying, patient, strong in soul, loving...To fight temptation, he urges prayer, obedience and evangelical joy in the Lord."[163]

At the end of his life, Francis asked Brother Leo to randomly open the Bible three times and all three times it opened to Christ's Passion. Then, Francis understood that there was nothing for him but to suffer to the end, and that his days of good fortune were gone for ever. And he resigned himself to God's will.

We all know how his dying body was carried to St. Clare's monastery in Assisi and of the lamentation of the people at the death of the man who was probably the most extraordinary saint of all times.

The Witness of Blessed Angela of Foligno

One of the most fascinating of women saints was Blessed Angela of Foligno.[164] Angela was born in 1248 of well-to-do parents. She was married in 1270 and had several sons. She is said to have been rich, proud, beautiful, fiery, passionate and impetuous. She enjoyed the comforts and luxuries of the world, and would later describe herself at this period of her life as superficial, pleasure-seeking, and adulterous. After her conversion in 1285 on a pilgrimage to Assisi, Angela tried to embark on the path of penance.

It was difficult for Angela to pursue holiness when her immediate family and relatives were all so worldly. Then, apparently because of a plague, all Angela's immediate family died suddenly. Grieving, Angela joined the Third Order of St. Francis in 1291. Angela was gifted with extraordinary mystical graces in the little cell she devised for herself after slowly and with difficulty giving away her possessions. Soon there were followers, men and women. Her instructions to them, a record of her own experiences and insights, were transcribed by her spiritual director. I selected the following quotations from what was written in her later years, from forty-eight to sixty-one.[165]

Before you continue reading, I should mention a truism about the writings of the mystics. If you are not prepared by the Holy Spirit to meditate on such truths, they will appear either exaggerated or simply boring. To get the most out of these excerpts and others to follow, I suggest you pray first and ask that whatever you need to learn may shine forth for you.

"Humility of heart is the matrix in which all the other virtues and virtuous works are engendered and from which they spring...This humility of heart that the God-man wished us to learn from him is a life-giving and clear light which opens the understanding of the soul so that it perceives both its own vileness and nothingness and the immensity of the divine goodness.

"The more the soul realizes the magnitude of the divine goodness, the more it advances in the knowledge of itself. The more it perceives and knows that it is nothing, the more it will rise up to know and praise the ineffability of the divine goodness which its humility makes it perceive and understand so fully. And from this, all other virtues begin to blossom..."[166]

"Truly, the soul thus transformed loves, with the love of God, every creature as is fitting, because in every creature it perceives, understands and recognizes God's presence."[167]

"Try to live without cares and without any desire to be self-sufficient."[168]

"I (Jesus) would not withdraw my presence from anyone who wants to feel my presence deeply."[169]

"The soul cannot have true knowledge of God through its own efforts or by means of any created thing, but only by divine light and by a special gift of divine grace. I believe there is no quicker or easier way for the soul to obtain this divine grace from God, supreme Good and supreme Love, than by a devout, pure, humble, continual, and violent prayer."[170]

If you are reading this section hastily, you may not have noticed that last, surprising adjective "violent!" If you read the entire book of writings about Blessed Angela's experiences of God, you will understand the allusion to violence better, for this mystic was known for the passion of her penitential "assault" on God. Always, she was begging Christ to fulfill the longings of her heart for salvation and union with Him at the same time as she was undergoing severe penances for her sins.

Angela's last letter before her final illness, written in 1308, includes these consoling words about what she called the seven gifts bestowed on us by the goodness of God. Amidst truths with which you are probably familiar, if you read closely you will find quite remarkable thoughts.

On the seven gifts

"The first is the ineffable gift of creation.

"The second is the wonderful election by which you have deigned to choose us to be in your presence.

"The third is the inestimable gift you bestowed on us when you sent your son to his death in order to give us life. This is the gift of gifts.

"The fourth is the highest gift of your goodness: you deigned to make me a sensible and rational creature, not an irrational beast. O admirable one, the power of reason which you have placed in me does three things for me. First, it makes me know you, the admirable one! Second, it makes me know my sins. Third, this same power of reason, which is mine by your grace, makes me oppose evil with my free will...

"The fifth is the gift of understanding. Make me worthy, Lord, to know this gift, for you have given it to us so that we may know you, my God.

"The sixth is the gift of wisdom. O Lord, make me worthy to know the most ardent charity with which you have given us this gift of your wisdom. Oh, in truth, this is the gift of gifts: to savor you in truth.

"The seventh gift is love. O supreme Being, make me worthy to understand this gift, which is greater than any other gift. For all the angels and the saints have no other gift than that of seeing you, their Beloved, and loving you and contemplating you. O gift above all other gifts, because you are that gift and you are love. O highest good, you have made us to know you, love itself, and make us love such love.

"All those who come into your presence will be satisfied according to the love they have. Nothing leads contemplatives to contemplate, except true love. O admirable one, you have done wonders in your sons! O supreme Good! O incomprehensible and most burning charity! O divine person, you have deigned to sustain us within your own substance! O, this is a wonder above all wonders that you have accomplished for your sons!...It is the pledge granted specifically to those who are true solitaries. It is the occupation of all the choirs of angels. And those who are true contemplatives are occupied in this way. Afterward they become solitaries and are separated from the earth. Their conversation is in heaven."[171]

During Angela's final illness which lasted five months, she wanted to receive Communion on the Feast of Angels, and there was no one to bring It. Then her soul was elevated to the altar of angels where God was being praised, and the angels told her she was in union with him.

Near the Feast of the Nativity, Angela "passed away to Christ." (What follows are excerpts from the words she said during her last week on earth. I have included them all with only *one* footnote to mark the place in the book from which I am quoting to avoid the annoyance of so many notes for what is really best read, it seems to me, as one undivided sequence.[172]

"Oh, every creature is found wanting! Oh, the intelligence of the angels is likewise not enough!"

Later she said, "Behold, the moment has arrived in which my God fulfills his promise to me. Christ, his Son, has now presented me to the Father...You know how when Christ was in the boat, there were great storms? Truly, it is sometimes like that with the soul. He permits storms to assail it, and he seems to sleep...In truth, God at times allows a person to be completely broken and downtrodden before he puts an end to the storm..."

"On another occasion, Angela said that her soul had been washed, cleansed, and immersed in the blood of Christ, which was fresh and warm as if it flowed from the body of Christ on the cross. Then it was said to my soul: 'This is what cleansed you.' And my soul replied: 'My God, will I be deceived?' 'No,' she was told.

"My soul then heard these words: 'O my spouse, my beautiful one, I love you with great affection. I do not want you to come to me burdened with these pains and sorrows, but jubilant and filled with ineffable joy. For it is only fitting for a king to wed his long-loved bride, clothed in royal garments.' He showed me the robe which the bridegroom shows to the bride he has loved for so long. This robe was neither of purple, nor of scarlet, nor of sendal, nor of samite, but of some marvelous light which clothed her soul.

"Then God showed me the Word, so that now I would understand what is meant by the Word and what it is to speak the Word. And he said to me: 'This is the Word who wished to incarnate himself for you.' At that very moment the Word came to me and went all through me, touched all of me, and embraced me.

"Before this, he had also said: 'Come to me, my beloved, my beautiful one, my dearest, whom I love so much. Come, for all the saints are waiting for you with great joy.' And he added: 'I do not entrust to either the angels or any other saints the task of bringing you to me. I will come for you in person and I will take you with me.' A long time before this he had also said: 'You have become suitable to be with me and have attained a most high place before my majesty.'

"On another occasion she said: 'Cursed be the advantages in life which inflate the soul: power, honor, and ecclesiastical office! My little children, strive to be small.'

"And then she cried out: 'O unknown nothingness! O unknown nothingness! Truly, a soul cannot have a better awareness in this world than to perceive its own nothingness and to stay in its own cell. There is greater deception in spiritual advantages than in temporal ones — that is, to know how to speak about God, to do great penances, to understand the Scriptures, and to have one's heart almost constantly preoccupied with spiritual matters. For those who are taken by them fall many times into errors and are more difficult to lead back to the right than those who have temporal advantages. And again she cried out: O unknown nothingness! O unknown nothingness!'

"When she was near death, the very day before she died, she frequently said: 'Father into your hands I commend my soul and my spirit.' One time, after she said this, she told us: 'I have just received this answer to what I said: That which is imprinted on your heart in life, it is impossible not to have in death.' Then we asked her: 'Do you want to go away and leave us?' She replied: 'I have kept it hidden from you, but now no longer. I must go.'

"That very day, all her suffering ceased. For many days before she had been horribly tormented and afflicted in every single part of herself, internally and externally. But now her body lay in such a state of rest and her soul in such happiness that she seemed to taste already some of the joy promised to her. We asked her then if this promised state of jubilation had indeed been granted to her. And she responded that, true enough, she was already in this said joy-filled state. She remained lying with her body and mind at rest and in a jubilant mood until Saturday night after Compline. She was surrounded by many friars who celebrated Divine Office in her presence. It was during the last hour of that day, on the octave of the Feast of the Holy Innocents that, as if gently falling asleep, she died peacefully.

"Thus, her most holy soul, freed from the flesh and absorbed into the abyss of divine charity, received from Christ, her spouse, the stole of immortality and innocence to reign with him forever. Where she is, may we too be led by the power of the most holy cross, the merits of Christ's most holy mother, and the intercession of our most holy mother, Angela, by Jesus Christ himself, the Son of God, who lives and reigns with the Father and the Holy Spirit, forever and ever. Amen."[173]

When it is time for me to leave this world, might my passing have even a smidgen of this glory?

The Witness of St. Teresa of Avila

One of the best known of women saints is St. Teresa of Avila, founder of the Reform Carmelite Order in 16th century Spain. She was born on March 28, 1515, and died on October 4, 1582.[174]

The aches and pains of old age were no surprise to Teresa since she had been ill for decades before. As a young nun she was treated by a medical quack for an undisclosed illness and left an invalid and paralytic for three years until cured through the intercession of St. Joseph. Because of this "she suffered the rest of her life from miserable health, a wide variety of illnesses. Antonio Aguiar, after his medical examination of Teresa when she was sixty-seven and nearing the end of her life, claimed that it was impossible to find the focal cause of her illnesses because her body had become a whole arsenal of ailments."[175]

Here are some excerpts from Teresa's writings about old age and death.

"At another time something else happened to me that frightened me very much. I was at a place where a certain person died who for many years had lived a wicked life, from what I knew. But he had been sick for two years, and in some things it seems he had made amends. He died without confession, but nevertheless it didn't seem to me he would be condemned.

"While the body was being wrapped in its shroud, I saw many devils take that body; and it seemed they were playing with it and punishing it. This terrified me, for with large hooks they were dragging it from one devil to the other.

"I was half stupefied from what I had seen. During the whole ceremony I didn't see another devil. Afterward when they put the body in the grave, there was such a multitude of them inside ready to take it that I was frantic at the sight of it, and there was need for no small amount of courage to conceal this. I reflected on what they would do to the soul when they had such dominion over the unfortunate body.

"May it please the Lord that what I have seen — a thing so frightful! — will be seen by all those who are in such an evil state; I think it would prove a powerful help toward their living a good life. All of this gives me greater knowledge of what I owe God and of what He freed me from."[176]

Here is a story with a happier ending:

"As soon as I learned he ('a person of many virtues') was dead, I felt a lot of disturbance because I feared for his salvation in that he had been a superior for twenty years. Being a superior is something I am indeed very afraid of since I think having souls in one's charge involves a lot of danger; with much anxiety I went to an oratory. I offered up for him all the good I had done in my life, which must in fact amount to little, and so I asked the Lord to supply from His own merits what was necessary for that soul to be freed from purgatory.

"While beseeching the Lord for this as best I could, it seemed to me that person came out from the depths of the earth at my right side and that I saw him ascend to heaven with the greatest happiness. He had been well advanced in years, but I saw him as only about thirty, or even less I think, and his countenance was resplendent."[177]

The following comes from *Soliloquies* written in 1569 when St. Teresa was fifty-four years old:

"Woe is me, woe is me, Lord, how very long is this exile! And it passes with great sufferings of longing for my God! Lord, what can a soul placed in this prison do? O Jesus, how long is the life of man, even though it is said to be short! It is short, my God, for gaining through it a life that cannot end; but it is very long for the soul that desires to come into the presence of its God. What remedy do You provide for this suffering? There isn't any, except when one suffers for You...

"O my Happiness and my God, what shall I do to please You? Miserable are my services, even though I may have rendered many to my God. Why, then, must I remain in this miserable wretchedness? That the will of the Lord may be done. What greater gain, my soul? Wait, wait, for you know neither the day nor the hour. Watch with care, for everything passes quickly, even though your desire makes the certain doubtful and the short time long. Behold the more you struggle the more you show the love you have for your God and the more you will rejoice in your Beloved with a joy and delight that cannot end."[178]

The following are quotations from William Thomas Walsh's biography of St. Teresa.[179] I will recount here only mention of the years from age fifty-nine to her death, from pages 429 to the end of Walsh's text. I imagine, like myself, the reader will enjoy the inimitable style of the saint:

"I am so old and tired you would be shocked to see me," wrote Teresa to her niece when she was fifty-nine.

During this year she continued to write letters to relatives, friends, and members of the Order...by means of bilocation she was able to be present to a sister dying full of anxieties and scruples. As a result of Teresa's "presence," this nun died alert and happy the next day. Also in this year, she was able to found new convents, traveling around Spain in "rude carts covered to protect from sun...traveling on ancient roads full of mud. They went to daily Mass along the way and every time they passed a small village church she got out and prostrated herself before it, saying, "What a great blessing that we should find here the Person of the Son of God! Wretched are those who drive Him from themselves!" On the last day of this journey, they got lost in the mountains and Teresa told the eight nuns traveling with them to pray to God and to St. Joseph — an old man (Teresa said he was her father Saint Joseph) yelled at them to stop and they did — if they had continued they would have gone over a precipice.

During one of these trips to Sevilla the band of Carmelites "had nothing to eat in two or three days except salty sardines and little or no water. They had been lead to believe that they would have decent lodgings, but it was very sparse — not even a rope for the well. They lived on a little bread and apples. Eventually the Archbishop allowed her to open the convent and a wealthy lady gave them food, clothing and money.

During the next few years Teresa suffered many persecutions from enemies within the church and also such loud noises in her head that she could not write. Not liking to be idle, the nun "went about her duties humbly, cheerfully and perfectly — wore old patched habits, and kept them very clean. Even while talking and listening, she did some sewing or knitting." At age sixty-one, Teresa wrote some of her greatest books. When asked to write more, she said, "I wish they would let me spin my flax, follow my choir and duties of religion, like the other sisters, for I am not fit for writing, nor have I health nor head for it."

In her early sixties, one Christmas Eve Teresa became dizzy on her way to Compline and fell down the stairs breaking her left arm. She always insisted that the devil had done it. "God help me," she cried as she lay at the bottom, "he tried to kill me!" And she heard a voice say, "He did, but I was with thee." There was no one to set it, so months later it was broken and reset — Teresa endured excruciating torments. After that she moved her hand a little, but the arm was never much good, and to the day of her death she was unable to dress or undress without help.

At the age of sixty-three she usually worked until one or two in the morning. Then she would get up before sunrise. So terrible was the persecution of her priestly friends during this time that she would weep for hours thinking all her work on the reform of the Carmelites would come to nothing. She lived to see the Order approved by Pope Gregory XIII.

In November, 1579, Teresa had a stroke of either paralysis or palsy and a heart attack, but was on the road again before fully recovering. She gave orders like a sea captain, performed prodigies of labor, fell on her knees and asked pardon if her sharp tongue offended anyone. Perfect health seemed hers those busy days; it was not until all was done that her fever and pains returned and she had to continue travels with a secretary to help her. During this time many of her friends died of a flu. In visions, Teresa saw many of these appearing in glory with God, Mary and/or Joseph in Heaven. Humorously she wrote of the death of a beloved brother:

"I rejoice that he has left this life of misery and is now in safety. Life passes so quickly that we ought to think more of how to die than how to live...I am four years older than my brother, yet I never manage to die."

In August, 1580, Teresa came down with the flu and was so sick the nuns thought she would die. Up to now she looked quite young — despite illnesses, fasts, vigils, scourges and incredible labors — "her cheek unwrinkled and her black eyes youthful." But now she looked like an old woman.

We wonder. Would Jesus really want this sick old nun to keep traveling? It seems He did. When Teresa thought about omitting a trip to Burgos thinking of the bitter cold there in the winter and of her own infirmities, Christ said to her: "Never mind the cold, I am the true warmth. Satan is exerting all his strength to hinder the foundation: do thou exert thyself on My behalf that it may be made, and go thyself without fail, for the fruits of it will be great."

And so, Teresa set off from Avila for the last time. It was the most dangerous trip she'd ever made — the rains were terrible, there were floods and washed out roads. They had to walk along the river and were almost dumped into the river. She insisted on being in the first cart so that if anyone drowned, it would be her. They had to cross the river on pontoons which were almost submerged. She'd had a fever and a very swollen throat, but when she opened her mouth for communion, "her tongue was loosed..." She was so wet and chilled that she sat up all night by the fire without being able to get warmed through, the smoke made her ill; her head grew dizzy, and she began to vomit and spit up blood with such violence that a wound opened in her throat. One of her most disgusting trials from then on was the frequent emergence of her voice, not through her half-paralyzed mouth, but through he gaping aperture in her neck.

The next day she was unable to get out of bed. When she learned that...important persons were coming to welcome her to Burgos, she had herself carried on a couch to a window opening on a corridor, and there through a curtain, she carried on her business as usual.

In July, 1582, she left for Avila. She stopped in Valladolid only to have her whole family against her concerning using her brother's legacy to build a chapel. The family told Teresa to get out and never come back to their house. As her biographer continues:

"So the 'old hag' took to the roads again, sick of body and heart...When she reached Alba she was so tired she went straight to bed saying: 'God help me, how tired I am; but I haven't been to bed this early in twenty years.'" She was up for Mass the next day and from then on till September 29th, when "she had a hemorrhage after Mass which left her so weak that she had to be helped back into bed in the infirmary. She had asked to be placed there so that she could look through a certain window and see the priest saying Mass in the chapel beyond."

"All that summer, the sisters at Alba had noticed strange lights shining in the choir, and sometimes at night heart something like a hushed but very distinct sigh passing through the corridors and cells. Now they began to understand the significance of all this. It was evident that Madre Teresa was going very soon to meet His Majesty face to face.

"Teresa spent all of the first night of October in prayer, and at dawn asked to have Fray Antonio of Jesus hear her confession. The first friar of her Reform was evidently much moved as he went in to hear the last self-accusation of a pure and virginal soul. The word went around the house that Christ had told her she was about to die. Some sisters told her afterward they had heard Fray Antonio say he would ask our Lord not to take her yet. 'Never mind about that,' said Teresa. 'I am no longer needed int his world.' The nuns all gathered at the bedside that day, and received her last counsels.

"On October 3, the eve of Saint Francis, at about five o'clock, she asked for *Viaticum*. The nuns dressed her in her veil and white choir mantle, and lighted holy tapers in the infirmary. She was so weak that they had to turn her in the bed. While they waited for the priest, each holding a lighted candle, La Madre began to speak: Hijas mias y senoras mias, for the love of God I beg that you will take great care with the keeping of the rule and Constitutions, and pay no attention to the bad example that this wicked nun has given you, and pardon me for it."

"When the priest arrived with the Blessed Sacrament, and she became aware that her lord was entering the room, she raised her body on the bed without any help, as though to throw herself on the floor. The nuns who held her down noticed that a change had come over her countenance: it was beautiful and illuminated beyond description, much younger than her age warranted. 'And clasping her hands, full of joy this swan of utter whiteness began to sing at the end of her life more sweetly than they had ever heard her sing, and spoke lofty things, amorous and sweet. Among others she said, 'Oh my Lord and my Spouse, now the desired hour is come. Now it is time for us to go. *Senor mio*, now is the time to set forth, may it be very soon, and may Your most holy will be accomplished! Now the hour has come for me to leave this exile, and my soul rejoices at one with You for what I have so desired!"

"She gave many thanks for having been a daughter of the Church and for dying in it. Over and over she repeated it: 'In short, Lord, I am a daughter of the Church...I am a daughter of the Church.' She spoke again of pardon for her sins, asked the nuns to pray for her again begged them to keep her Rule...

"She was in great pain during the night, but from time to time could be heard praying and singing. The next morning, October 4, she turned suddenly on one side 'like Mary Magdalen in the paintings,' and holding a crucifix tightly in her hand, remained perfectly still, as some of them had seen her in the prayer of union or in rapture; and thus she lay, motionless, ecstatic, until evening, except at one time when she made little signs as if speaking earnestly with someone. At nine o'clock in the evening the precise moment; it was just as they had often seen her in the highest prayer. Her face was gloriously young and beautiful. The little sigh that escaped her lips was like the sound they had heard so many nights during the summer.

"Many strange things occurred at her passing. A brilliant star had been noticed just over the church every evening between eight and nine. Crystal rays of colored light passed the window of the infirmary cell where she was to die. Shortly before she went, Blessed Ana de San Bartolome saw our Lord at the foot of the bed in majesty and splendor, attended by myriad angels, and at the head, the Ten Thousand Martyrs who had promised Teresa, in a rapture years before, to come for her in the moment of death.

"When she sighed her last, one of the sisters saw something like a white dove pass form her mouth. And while Sister Catalina de la Concepcion, who was very holy and had less than a year to live, was sitting by the law window opening on the cloister by La Madre's cell, she heard a great noise as of a throng of joyful and hilarious people making merry, and then saw innumerable resplendent persons, all dressed in white, pass the cloister and into the room of the dying Saint, where the nuns gathered about her seemed but a handful in comparison; and then all advanced toward the bed. And this was the moment when Teresa died."

"When she died her skin was like that of a three year old — all wrinkles gone. Her body and everything that touched it had a sweet smell."

Much as I loved reading of the glorious death of my favorite woman saint, I would like to end this witness of St. Teresa of Avila, Doctor of the Church, with something she herself wrote at the age of sixty-six, a year before her death, describing her state of soul:

"Oh, who would be able to explain...the quiet and calm my soul experiences! It is so certain it will enjoy God that it thinks it already enjoys the possession of him, although not the fruition. It's as though one had given another, with heavily warranted deeds, the promise of a large revenue that the other will be able to enjoy at a certain time. But until then, this latter person enjoys only the promise that he shall have the fruition of this revenue. Despite the gratitude the soul feels, it would rather not rejoice. For it thinks it hasn't deserved anything other than to serve, even if this service be through much suffering. And sometimes it even seems to it that the period from now until the end of the world would be a short time to serve the one who gave it this possession.

"Because...the soul is like a lord in his castle and so it doesn't lose its peace; although this security doesn't remove a great fear of offending God and of not getting rid of all that would be a hindrance to serving Him. The soul rather proceeds more cautiously, but it goes about so forgetful of self that it thinks it has partly lost its being. In this state everything is directed to the honor of God, to the greater fulfillment of His will, and to His glory.

"As a great sacrifice (the soul) offers Him the care it takes of its body, and this care wearies it very much...

"I sometimes feel fear, although not with pain and disturbance as before, that my soul is in a stupor and that I am doing nothing because I cannot do penance...It seems I live
only to eat and sleep and not suffer in anything; and even
this doesn't bother me, although sometimes, as I say, I fear
lest I be deceived. But I'm not able to believe that I am, because form all that I can discern there doesn't reign in me
any strong attachment to any creature or to all the glory of
heaven, but rather to loving this God of ours. This attachment to loving God doesn't diminish; instead, in my opinion, it increases along with the desire that all serve Him...

"If I were now to strive with great care to desire to die, I
wouldn't be able to. Nor would I be able to make the acts I
used to, or feel the suffering over offenses aginst God, or
feel the fears that were so great and that I bore for so many
years becuase it seemed to me I was being deceived. And as
a result I no longer have any need to seek out learned men
or tell any one anything. I only need the satisfaction of
knowing whether I am going along all right...

"...the interior peace, and the lack of strength that pleasures or displeasures have for taking this peace away in any
lasting manner...

"The presence of the three Persons is so impossible to
doubt that it seems one experiences what St. John says, that
they will make their abode in the soul. God does this not
only by grace but also by His presence, because He wants to
give the experience of this presence. It brings with it an
abundance of indescribable blessings, especially the blessing that there is no need to go in search of reflections in order to know that God is there.

"This presence is almost continual, except when a lot of
sickness weighs down on one. For it sometimes seems God
wants one to suffer without interior consolation; but never,
not even in its first stirrings, does the will turn from desire
that God's will be done in it.

"This surrender to the will of God is so powerful that the soul wants neither death nor life, unless for a short time when it longs to die to see God. But soon the presence of the three Persons is represented to it so forcefully that this presence provides a remedy for the pain caused by His absence, and there remains the desire to live, if He wills, in order to serve Him more. And if through my intercession I could play a part in getting a soul to love and praise God more, even if it be for just a short time, I think that would matter more to me than being in glory."[180]

The Witness of St. Alphonsus Liguori

When doing research for my book *Kiss from the Cross: A saint for Every Kind of Suffering*, I read a long biography of this 18th century Doctor of the Church. Going through the chapters about his last years as a ninety-year old, I remember thinking that he was a wonderful model for overcoming terrible problems of aging. So I was happy to see that someone else had the same idea years ago and came out with a booklet called "Autumn Memoirs of St. Alphonsus Liguori."[181]

Declared patron of moral theologians by Pius XII, Liguori was most well-known in the nineteenth and early twentieth century for his writings on theological problems of pastors and confessors. Originally he wanted to be a lawyer, but eventually gave into the tug of a vocation to the priesthood. He was the founder of the Redemptorists — a congregation of priests and brothers living a common life in imitation of Christ and giving missions mainly in poor areas. He was made bishop at age sixty-six. His best known books in our time are *The Glories of Mary* and *Visits to the Blessed Sacrament*.

I was interested to read in the booklet that Liguori was fond of the writings of St. Teresa of Avila, particularly concerning suffering and the cross. In the booklet "Autumn Reflections," the Redemptorist priest author pretends that he is old Liguori reflecting on this life. Here are some excerpts from this imaginative document. I quote from it instead of from the actual writings of the saint because it seems to me to be easy to take in this form:

"The problem of suffering, pain, and the cross is one of the most difficult problems with which we Christians have to wrestle. I know that I have been wrestling with it for many years. Some of my friends tease me by reminding me that I am only getting what I have asked for all these years. They are referring to something in a small booklet of prayers for the fourteen Stations of the Cross I wrote many years ago. The last line in each of the fourteen prayers is: 'Grant that I may love thee always and then do with me whatever thou will.'

"My friends point out that over and over again I have given God a free hand to do with me *whatever* he wished, and yet, as soon as some suffering comes I so easily fall into depression and begin to complain, if not to him then at least to everybody else. It is true, this little prayer is one of the most difficult to say if you really mean what you are saying. It could be that on the very day you assure God that you want to give him an absolutely free hand, he might just be in the market for a victim soul to carry some special cross for the redemption of a poor sinner who is too weak to carry the cross himself. That is the kind of spirituality that has kept me relatively sane during all these years of suffering: I can actually endure this cross for someone else's spiritual benefit."[182]

What were the physical sufferings Alphonsus endured? From childhood he had poor eyesight and asthma. This was particularly difficult for him because his father was a robust seaman who despised his son for being frail.

Here are the words his biographer used to express Liguori's long list of sufferings while aging:

"If I had to set a date, I would say that my real agony in the garden, health-wise, started in my mid-fifties. What began as a simple catarrh, a congestion of the nose, throat, and chest, wound up as a serious blockage of the lungs with accompanying pains in the chest. Then came the constant headaches and fevers.

"When I was 66, the doctors had just about given up; they told me quite frankly that I was mortally ill and should prepare to meet my Maker. I am sure it was not the doctors who pulled me through that crisis. In all probability, the good nuns were to blame for that. I say *blame* because I was prepared to die and would truly have been happy to have departed this life even then. Mind you, the fact that I did not die does not mean that I was cured. By no means. You can imagine my shock when, later that same year, the Holy Father made me bishop of St. Agatha of the Goths, despite all my protestations of poor health.

"I spent most of my thirteen years as a diocesan bishop either in a wheel chair or a bed. Even when I could stumble around the diocese I had to use two canes or else be supported on either side by two stout clerics. My diocese was at a rather high elevation in the hills northeast of Naples where the winters can be brutally damp and cold. Each winter I would wind up in bed for a month at a time, struggling with the asthma or the recurring rheumatic arthritis. Winters always were a time of special agony for me.

"In the years '66 through '68, I was anointed and received the Viaticum at least once, and sometimes twice a year. In '67 malaria was added to my litany of maladies. The fevers had me out of my head for weeks on end. The poor doctors did not know what to do next. They tried hot compresses and cold compresses; then they started to bleed me again; then came the purges with all sorts of herbs and foul-smelling concoctions. When the fevers went away, the sciatica took over. It seemed to have settled in my hips and my back — all of this in addition to the rheumatism which had already twisted and tortured both legs and spine.

"As I look back, I would have to say that 1769 was the year that my wretched health dealt me the unkindest blow of all. I say this because for one whole year I couldn't celebrate the Holy Sacrifice of the Mass at all. You have no idea what a cross that is for a priest. Before that happened I had to give up saying the Divine Office because of my poor vision; now I was deprived of the consolation of saying mass. God help me; I was pretty near despair that year.

"Besides all that, there was the embarrassment of having the clergy and the laity, who came to the bishop's house on business, see their bishop lying in bed or strapped to a chair, his body twisted and deformed like some hideous gnome. As often as not I had to be wheeled out of the room in the middle of an interview with some *monsignore* or *barone* because I would be gagging on the blood which hemorrhaged from my lungs during most of that year.

"The medical profession was at a loss as to how to explain my survival. Thank God the doctors of my diocese were good and compassionate men; in their pity they even stopped charging me for their services. Years before, I had written to all the Superiors in my Congregation that we would sell even our books and chalices to take care of the sick, but this was not necessary in St. Agatha's. The medical men there were veritable saints. I know for certain that my constant need for their professional care made them even greater saints; perhaps it would be better to call them martyrs of patience, as they surely needed patience with my decaying body. God bless them all wherever they are today!

"Most of the time I could not see their faces as I was so bent in two with the sciatica and arthritis. Indeed, I was beginning to wear a raw and livid hole in my chest with the pointed bone of my chin. Every once in a while I would let a teardrop fall on my coverlet, so tender was the love and pity of those medical men.

"About eight years ago, I think it was in 1772, even my heart began to rebel at the burden it had to carry. In the middle of the night I would cry out in pain at the terrible tightness and the dagger-like stabs of pain in my chest. The doctors called it 'irregular heart palpitation' and finally decided that it was a kind of repetitive heart failure. I suppose the gradual filling of the lungs, plus the internal bleeding, was more than my heart could handle, and so it too began to lie down on the job along with the rest of my vital organs.

"In 1773 I almost died again! One night I heard the clergy of my household holding a whispered discussion of the names of the *monsignori* who were waiting in line to jump into my episcopal boots at my demise.

"How can I ever give a rational explanation to you for the Pope's refusal to accept my resignation? Like the old lady in the Gospel, I kept banging at the door of the master of the household, but like the master in the Gospel parable, the Holy Father kept saying: 'Go away and leave me alone. Stop bothering me.' However, perseverance always wins. In 1775, the pope broke down and permitted me to resign my See. I was as ecstatic as any dying man could be...

"Here it is five years later and this old curmudgeon goes on and on. The students like to give me birthday parties. Of course, they do all the partying while I must sit and watch. At each party I solemnly assure them that this particular one will absolutely, positively be my last. Do you know what they do then? They laugh and laugh! I suppose they have a right to laugh since I have been predicting my final departure for the last thirty years. The young students insist I will live to be one hundred. Please God, let them be wrong!

"Before I end this section, which has been one long tale of woe, let me tell you a funny story about homecoming. Remember how I told you that I was practically bent in half? Well, during the first few weeks back I was in such pain that they couldn't get me into bed. I had to sleep strapped in my wheelchair, and even awake my eyes saw nothing but my feet and the floor. Finally, the pain eased a bit and they decided to put me into bed. It took several Brothers and students to lift me from the chair and maneuver me into the bed.

"As soon as I slid onto the mattress I let out a blood-curdling shriek: 'Ah, what have you idiots done?' Well, the poor fellows stood there petrified. They thought that perhaps they had broken my spinal column or maybe torn the dried ulcers on my body. Heh, heh, heh! What happend was simply this: when they put me flat on the bed, I saw for the first time, the outlandish job they had done in decorating and gilding the ceiling of my cell so as to make it more worthy of a retired bishop of the Church. *Stupidoni*. What a good waste of money all to honor nothing more than an episcopal skeleton almost ready for burial. I ranted and raged for at least five minutes, so much so that they were afraid I would have a heart attack or a stroke. I guess their hearts were in the right place; they really meant well!

"That night, as I lay there squinting at the baroque monstrosity of a ceiling, I decided that I had better get Vilanni for forgiveness for my temper tantrum over something so ridiculous. But the look on their faces when I screamed was truly hilarious. Now I can laugh about the whole thing but the times of joy and laughter during these years of suffering are few and far between. I do not think I could have carried the cross for so long had it not been for prayer. In fact, the thought just struck me that I have not told you anything about my views on prayer. We shall never get safely through this life or into the next life of eternal happiness without prayer. But I shall save some thoughts about that for my next entry.

"I have written this whole section a few lines at a time and some I dictated to the Brother or one of the students. If it has been slightly disconnected it is because that is the way my thoughts are in these twilight years. It is time for bed and I shall have to lie beneath that awful ceiling again. Thank God, I cannot see it clearly and won't have to contemplate the mediocre art. It is enough to give a person nightmares. *Good-night!*

"When I was young, I resented it when people talked about old folks as being in their second childhood. Bad enough to get old, but worse to be labeled with a term that implies that one is a baby again, with all the helplessness that goes along with it. However, now that I am eighty-four, plus a few months, I think I know what second childhood is all about.

"In many ways, old age is often the last indignity of life, especially when one has become as utterly helpless as I have. At least a baby feels no embarrassment or shame at being bathed, fed, combed, and even accompanied to the bathroom. I would dare say that the great virtue of old age has to be humility. There is little I can do without asking for help.

"Today, for example, I am dictating all these words, and that with great difficulty. Just the other day I was saying to Villani that all I can do is sit here and pray all day. Spiritual man that he is, he answered that all my running around and all my writing these many years are as nothing compared to the power of prayer. That seems to ring a bell in my head. Maybe Villani is quoting me, rubbing my nose in some of my own pious sentiments. I feel sure I have said the same thing to others.

"Now that I am old and dying, I think that God is doing a magnificent job of purifying my soul. The masters of the spiritual life would call it the process of spiritual aridity. The only reason I am mentioning this personal trial of mine at all is because I am trying to be helpful. I have found that so many people suffer terrible anguish and pain and yet never recognize it for what it is, namely, the hand of the Lord purifying us for some special gift which he has in store for us.

"I have gone through this many times — first, the frightening dryness of spirit and afterward, the great gifts of joy and consolation. I used the word "frightening' advisedly. Where once prayer was a joy, now it becomes a burden. Where once there was confidence and trust, now there is only fear, distrust, and at times, a kind of despair. Sometimes the soul imagines that it really hates God and that, because of this, it is already damned.

"Finally, and worst of all, come all sorts of temptations against purity, doubts about faith, and a state of total depression. The amazing thing is that, even though the will resists all of this, the darkness is so deep that the poor soul wonders whether it is resisting at all. The only thing to do during this sad state of affairs is to hang on by one's teeth. Many years ago I wrote down, and now I pass on to you, a beautiful quotation from Saint Teresa which has been a great help to me in my periodic sieges of spiritual dryness. She wrote: 'By means of dryness and temptations, God tests his lovers. And even though the aridity should last a life time, if they do not give up mental prayer, the day will come when all will be repaid.' What a consoling thought for a person in desolation!

"I am hoping that my day of repayment will come soon! Since this tale of woe may have saddened you, I shall stop here; perhaps that will give you joy. I hope so! I simply am too tired to go on. I have a feeling that I shall have to put an end to these memoirs altogether in the not too distant future.

"This past year has also brought deep sorrow to my other family (other than his natural family — his youngest brother died), the Congregation of the Most Holy Redeemer. In September came the *Provisional Decree* of the Holy Father which separated the Roman Redemptorists from those of us who lived in the Kingdom of Naples. Since then we have had nothing but one grand diplomatic disaster after another.

"As of today, it looks as if I shall die under the frown of the Holy Father. I do not mind being stripped of my office

as Superior General — I did not want the job in the first
place — but it is the loss of our missionary privileges which
hurts me the most.

"And here I sit, wondering why God has allowed all of
this to happen to me, a dear old friend of his who has done
so much, for his Church in general and for the Holy See in
particular. It was not bad enough that I had to sit here rotting
away physically; now I am decaying mentally and emotionally. Sometimes I cry all through the long nights and the
dear Brother comes softly in and takes me in his arms like a
little child in need of comfort.

"Each night I pray to God to take me out of this wretched
world, but every dawn finds me still here, writhing in physical and mental torture with even my spirit in near despair.
Mine is a living death, I can call it nothing else. I ought to
be dragged through the streets for having let myself be
duped and for not having forced myself to read those docu-
ments word for word. What a pleasant punishment that
would be compared to my daily dragging through this valley of tears, darkness, and desolation, believe me when I say
that I am hanging onto my sanity by a mere thread. Yet, it
would be better to die insane than to die in despair. At the
moment both seem equally probably.

"Oh, compassionate Jesus, be merciful to me a sinner.
Mary, Mother of the Redeemer and my mother, let me not
be lost for all eternity. Saint Joseph, patron of a happy death,
at least let me die at peace with myself and with my brethren.

"Sweet Lord, let me say it one more time: "Grant that I
may love thee always, and then, do with me whatever thou
wilt." Amen, so do I hope, so may it be!"[183]

Alphonsus lived another six years — in increasing physical pain, and in and out of senility. But he continued in
prayer, which brought him a peaceful death. From heaven
he would have to see how his beloved Order flourished and

how many Catholics he helped through his writings and intercessory prayers.

The Witness of St. Elizabeth Seton

Whenever I am working on books about the saints, I love to come to our American saint, Elizabeth Ann Seton (1774-1821).[184] Partly it is because we can read her letters without translation and catch their homey style as we cannot so easily do with saints from other countries. Partly, I love to read her because she was a mother, a widow, and a late-vocation nun, roles I identify with easily.

Before offering you quotations that come from Elizabeth Seton's old age, I want you to read lines from her letters about the death of her children and relatives, for that is part of the pain of aging, to sometimes lose those you hoped would outlive you.

Here is how the widow wrote about the on-rushing death of one of her daughters:

"Eternity always at hand!...I look to the far, so far distant shore, the heaven of heavens — a few days more and Eternity — now then, all resignation...rest in him — the heart in sweet bitterness. Abandon."[185]

On the death of a sister in her order, Elizabeth wrote:

"What a moment, the greatest, the decisive moment of this Earth — the Soul passing to Eternity — happy Eternity for her! O my God! Silence and tears for us who remain in the land of our exile..."

Somewhat humorously, Elizabeth wrote in her journal about this death:

"Death of Sister Benedicta Extract from the Gazetter of Heaven 1814 or our Lord — Eternity — date immoveable.

"It is reported...the angel of Sister Benedicta is to bring her this night to the tribunal — her packages are already arrived...all the newcomers (those died recently before her) are looking earnestly for the coming of their dear Sister — and all the heavenly court take a part in their pleasure."

Then she wrote about three other sick members of the community: "Three poor lingering Souls are about to be let free and their mortal fetters are breaking so fast there is little doubt we must have them soon sharing our Joys. (They have been earnest about penance mending bad spots with the precious blood.)"

In 1812 Elizabeth's daughter Anna died and though she had dealt with other deaths of soul sisters very well with great hope, she would say of this death:

"After Nina was taken I was so often expecting to lose my senses and my head was so disordered that unless for the daily duties always before me I did not know much of what I did or what I left undone."

For six months Elizabeth was unconsolable. She wished she were dead, though she had two other daughters and two sons to live for. Her beloved confessor brought her to see that she had to accept God's will in this Providence. The longest life is nothing to eternity."

When her youngest daughter died, Elizabeth didn't feel the same kind of despair. Instead, she would rejoice to look at the cemetery and realize that the girl had no more pain, but only the joy of eternity.

An example of St. Elizabeth Seton's home theology is this quotation:

"The gate of Heaven is very low; only the humble can enter it."

Among her most famous sentences is this one:

"Eternity, eternity, when shall I come to You at last?...in eternity where we will love with a glance of the soul."

When Elizabeth herself was dying of tuberculosis she took the greatest solace from holy communion, but felt ever more undeserving. She thought of herself not as a sheep but as a dog who shouldn't eat the heavenly bread, surely Jesus would be able to see her canine qualities.

"Oh, Food of Heaven, how my soul longs for you with desire! Seed of Heaven, pledge of its immortality, of that eternity it pants for. Come, come my Jesus, bury yourself within my heart."

The saint's confessor said that her joy was great when given communion on her death bed.

"As I placed the ciborium upon the little table, she burst into tears and sobbing aloud covered her face with her two hands. I thought first that it was some fear of sin, and approaching her, I asked... 'Have you any pain? Do you wish to confess' 'No, no only give him to me,' as she said with an ardor, a kind of exclamation and her whose pale face was so inflamed that I was much affected and repeating 'Peace dear Mother, receive with great peace your God of peace'.... Among her last words when a sister wanted to give her a potion to relieve the pain, 'Never mind the drink,' she whispered 'One Communion more and then Eternity.'"

A few other words from Elizabeth may help us face our problems of aging:

"Mind not while in the body, what when out of the body you will have no need of."

"He who is idle is tempted by all devils at once."

"Why care for any thing personal if it *is*, or is *not*, *so*, or *not so*. The little remaining moment, all too little indeed for Penance much less reparation of love."

The Witness of Blessed Brother Andre

I would now like to jump to holy men and women who lived into the 20th century and have much to tell us about aging. My first witness is one of the most extraordinary men of the Church of our times, Brother Andre (1845-1937) of Montreal, Canada.[186]

Brother Andre came from an abjectly poor family with twelve children. As an adult he couldn't write anything but his name. He was an itinerant manual laborer who eventually became a Holy Cross brother. From his perch behind the counter of the Order's gift-shop, this less than 5' tall Brother Andre was reported to have been a conduit for more than 1,000 miraculous healings, all of which he attributed to the intercession of St. Joseph.

In the year 1909 Brother Andre was nearly sixty-four years old. He had served as doorkeeper of the College for nearly forty years, although in the last decade the number of menial tasks assigned to him had been considerably reduced as he gave increasing time to ministering to the sick and supervising the operation of the Oratory. Now Brother Andre could devote all eighteen hours of his workday to his mission. He moved his few possessions to a little shed near the chapel, where, after forty years of sleeping on a narrow bench, he was given a folding bed, as well as, wonder of wonders, a telephone![187]

At the age of nearly seventy, Brother Andre moved into a ministry that extended beyond the College and the Oratory. So many sick people confined to home or hospital requested the "miracle man" to come to them that the Superior decided to authorize Brother Andre to go on evening visits. At first, the Brother, who was sixty at the beginning of the automobile age and had never learned to drive, went on his calls by foot or trolley, but within a few years laymen were volunteering to drive him about in their cars.[188]

This change in Brother Andre's life illustrated for me that sometimes we think we have to give up some work as we age, but really all we need is more help in doing it.

His biographer describes Brother Andre in his seventies in this way:

"By this time Brother Andre was seventy-two years old. Most people had never known him as anything other than old. Yet there seemed to be an ageless quality in the spritely, elfin brother with his leathered face, his curly white hair, and penetrating dark eyes. A reporter left a striking word picture of Brother Andre in his seventies when he described: a man dressed in black, whose slight form was enveloped from shoulders to feet in a somber overcoat, standing at daybreak atop the steep staircase leading to the Crypt, raising his face to the splendor of the sunrise, and slowly extending his arms towards God in a gesture of adoration."[189]

Brother Andre's relatives described him as a very jolly and humble man, very pious, lively, down to earth, and warm — happy, cheerful, and confident. "Happiness comes from the Good God, sadness from the devil," he had a habit of saying. "It's not necessary to be sad...you have to laugh a little."

Considering all the physical ailments he had to endure, such advice is refreshing. Brother Andre suffered from headache, intestinal cramps, stomach pains, heartburn, constipation, heart problems — but he never prayed for healing for himself. He said that Christians should desire to endure their sufferings for the love of God without complaining.[190]

For example, concerning exhaustion he used to say, "It is good to suffer. It makes you think. You feel better after suffering..." He used to say to sufferers, "God will have eternity to console you. If you knew what reward awaits in heaven for the smallest suffering well borne, you would ask on your knees to suffer...suffering is a deposit in your account in heaven. After this life, you can claim it and benefit from it."[191]

He is reported to have been exquisitely soft and kind toward those who abused him. Even when very wrinkled in old age, when he smiled his face was illuminated with joy.

Brother Andre confessed to being impatient and in extreme old age he was said to be crotchety. I love this anecdote concerning a woman who had been healed of fainting fits by his administration of St. Joseph oils. The same woman was unwilling to wear her hateful dentures. "Tell her to wear her dentures! I surely can't wear them for her."[192]

Some thought that he could not be considered as a saint after his death because of his bad temper. But others pointed out that Brother Andre felt terrible when he hurt anyone, sometimes weeping over his temper.

Concerning heaven and whether one has to be perfect to get there, Brother Andre used to say: "When we do the best we can, we must have confidence in the good God. It would be an insult to Him if we believed that we would not go to heaven after we did our best. When one has lead a good life, death is not a thing to fear for it is the gate of heaven."[193]

When he was seventy-five and someone asked Brother Andre about his exhausting schedule he replied, "Old? I'm not old! Look you, seven and five makes twelve, which is to say I am twelve years old! Tired? Is ever one tired in the service of the Master?"[194]

At ninety-one years old he was constantly dizzy, nauseated, vomiting blood and experiencing excruciating chest pains, with abdomen swollen and bowels locked, yet never complained or talked about his condition. But he would lie in bed with an expression of sublime joy. He said that he could do much more for the Oratory in heaven than on earth. On his death bed in a hospital, he said, "One doesn't think about death enough...sickness is a good thing because it helps us reflect on our past life and make reparations through penitence and through suffering." After a violent attack of pain he said, "The Great Almighty is coming! Heaven is so beautiful that it is worth all the trouble with which one prepares for it...how beautiful God is, since the soul, which is but a ray of His beauty, is so lovely."[195]

Nearly a hundred thousand came from all over Canada and the United States to file by his open coffin! The healings go on.

The Witness of Ven. Louis Martin and Celine Martin

The stories of the old age of Little St. Therese of Lisieux's father and her sister, Celine, have a particular in-

terest for us because they mirror a common reality of our
times: an adult child taking care of an elderly parent and
then living to great old age herself. Information about them
comes from several biographical sources.[196]

Louis Martin was, of course, the widower father of the
family of holy girls of Lisieux. He was born 1823 and died
at sixty-six in 1889. As a young man he had tried the religious life unsuccessfully and married an equally devout
wife who had wanted to be a nun. Even though the couple
had to face the death of several of their little children, their
life in society and the Church seemed unusually happy until
the death of Zelie, Louis' wife, and then his unexpected,
catastrophic, progressive illness, sometimes identified as
Alzheimer's.

It was just before Celine was to enter the convent with so
many sisters already gone that "Her father showed alarming
signs of cerebral arteriosclerosis: forgetfulness, anxiety, and
hallucinations that, even though short-lived, made her
(Celine) fear more serious difficulties.

"He said he was prepared for an immediate separation
(Celine's entering the convent). 'You can all leave. I will be
happy to give you to God before I die. In my old age, a bare
cell will be enough for me.'

"His health continued to deteriorate; the old gentleman
found himself caught once again by his dreams of the er-
emitical life: to flee far from his family, in solitude, so that
his daughters could realize their destiny. Possessed by these
thoughts, he left Lisieux without warning on June 23, 1888.
After she had spent three days looking anxiously for him, a
telegram sent from Le Havre and asking for a reply to be
sent 'general delivery' enabled Celine and M. Guerin (her
uncle) to catch up with him and bring him home.

"When he suffered another attack, 'he experienced one
of his darkest days.' Celine's suffering was so great that
'while walking along the edge of the wharf, I looked with

envy into the depths of the water. Ah! If I did not have faith, I would be capable of anything.' She became calm at last in the love of Christ crucified.

"'No,' the holy daughter thought, 'I am not going to ask God to relieve me of the humiliations, misunderstandings, heartaches, anxieties, bitterness...But I do beg God to take all that away form our dear little father...'"

Finally, Louis Martin had to be put into a psychiatric institution. Close by, to be with him daily, were Celine and Leonie, the sister who tried many times, finally successfully, to enter the Visitation Convent.

Once a doctor said he was going to be cured. "Oh! I don't want that; I even ask God not to hear the prayers of those who make that intention, because this trial is a mercy. I am here to atone for my pride. I deserve the illness that has struck me down!"[197]

How touching these humble words concerning illness as necessary for the proud: "I have always been in the habit of commanding and now I am reduced to obedience, that is hard. But I know why the dear God gave me this trial; I have never had humiliation in my life, it was necessary for me to have one."[198]

During this long trial, Louis "was entirely resigned; he showed gentleness and an unfailing charity to those around — and received communion as often as possible."[199]

When her father was in the psychiatric hospital for three years, Celine wrote:

"The longer I live, the more I see exile on all sides. The world seems like a dream to me, immense confusion...The more I travel, and the more I see of things, the more detached I am from this earth, because, at each instant, the more I observe the nothingness of what passes away. I am in a real 'cell'; nothing pleases me more than this poverty. I would not exchange it for the most brilliant drawing room in the world." Her only happiness was in the chapel. "I want to be happy about our tribulations and to do even more; to thank God for the bitterness of our humiliations. I do not know why, but instead of receiving these trials with bitterness and complaint, I see something mysterious and divine in the conduct of our Lord toward us! Besides, did he himself not pass through all humiliations!"[200]

Celine sometimes burst forth in lamentation:

"How my poor heart is broken! I cannot get used to seeing our dear little father so ill. I always remember how it was at home, when he spoke to us like a true patriarch. He is so good!

"Oh! How God must love us in seeing us so afflicted! I ask myself why he is not impatient to call our beloved father to himself; it seems to me that he is making a great effort to leave him here on earth; some great good will have to come of it, both for his own glory as well as for papa and for us; without that, he could not wait so long...Dear little sisters, how happy we shall be when we are all reunited again on high! How these trials make us sigh for our heavenly home!"[201]

When Louis Martin's legs became paralyzed, they allowed him to be released from the psychiatric institution and returned to the care of Celine in Lisieux. The mind of Louis Martin was clear, but he could not speak because of the strokes. When he was leaving the parlour he pointed his index finger upward and said "in heaven."

Of that time, the daughter, Celine, wrote:

"I will always remember his beautiful face when, in the evening, as night fell in the deep woods, we stopped to hear a nightingale: he (L. Martin) listened...with what expression in his gaze! It was like an ecstasy, some inexpressible part of heaven was reflected in his features. Then after a good moment of silence, we were still listening, and I saw tears streaming down his dear cheeks. Oh! What a fine day."[202]

A month before he died, Louis was full of life, of understanding, tenderness and illuminated intelligence, and after his death the family of sisters felt his protection.

We now turn to the old age of Celine (1869-1959) who entered the Carmelite convent after the death of her father. I strongly recommend the biography called *Celine, Sister Genevieve of the Holy Face* by Fr. Stephane-Joseph Piat from which we have already been quoting concerning the old age of Louis Martin. I found the biography especially interesting because I have difficulty identifying with the character of my beloved Little Therese. In Celine I found the spirituality of Therese lived out by one whose temperament is more like mine.

"At 82, Sister Genevieve (Celine) expected to spend her time quietly being taken care of. However..."it was as if she had acquired a new youth, and the last phase of her life overflowed with activity. Her faculties, which remained intact, submitted to incessant labor, capable of crushing the most vigorous and mature temperament. This beautiful longevity...was nothing short of a miracle."

Not that the health of holy Celine was perfect. "From her thirties rheumatism deformed and stiffened her knees, shoulders, neck and jaw, by her seventies she had sciatica and gout — then stomach, liver, heart and lung problems, and later insomnia, and loss of hearing and eyesight."

Celine liked to joke about her infirmities: "It's always the same...A long illness wearies the doctor." She said she was like "a pincushion full of needles. Like Naaman, I would have to go and bathe seven times in the Jordan in order to regain my health.'" She referred to her infirmities as "ten leopards", the term Ignatius of Antioch used to describe his jailers. "What deficiencies in an old lady! What a procession of incapacities accompanies her! But how much profit must be in it since God allows them to exercise control over us, he who is so grieved to see us suffer."[203]

Still Celine, Sister Genevieve, at eight-three, half-numb, half-blind was continuing her work on the spirituality of Little Therese.

"She could be seen, at eighty-four years of age, toiling over a whole pile of papers with a magnifying glass, working up two booklets that appeared in 1953 and 1954, which were entitled: "The Father" and "The Mother of Saint Therese of the Child Jesus." After having drawn up the moral portrait of these noble Christians, Celine stressed their sickness and death. She also included in the appendix, along with a sketch, valuable topographical details of the house and the garden on the rue Saint-Blaise in Alençon. Those who witnessed this lengthy effort at clarification and composition were altogether edified by the youthful fervor and the strict historical integrity of this author."[204]

Three days after the celebration (a trial to her) of the 60th anniversary of her profession, she "suffered an attack of influenza that threatened her life. For six months, almost continuous suffering tormented her nights. She bore it peacefully, doing everything possible not to disturb her infirmarian. She was encouraged by thinking of the martyrs, especially Saint Sebastian, who, delivered miraculously from death, confronted his persecutor a second time and received the martyr's crown twice. 'It is incredible how God helps me,' she confided. 'I would never have wanted to ask him for suffering, but now I thank him.'

"Thus debilitated, it seemed that a new crisis would promptly overcome her. 'I have gone down into the valley of the shadow of death,' she wrote. 'Truthfully, I fear nothing about it, and I am quite abandoned to it without being conscious of it.' Contrary to all expectations, she rallied. Toward the end of April when, for the second time, the general assembly of the Federation of the French Carmels met at Lisieux, she again had to receive some two hundred and sixty superiors and delegates who were permitted to visit the interior of the monastery. She consented to this stream of visitors with good grace, careful, despite her fatigue, to give each one a personal mark of interest."[205]

In 1957, when Celine was 88, the Bishop decided to
open the cause for the canonization of her father. Celine
wanted this only if her parents could be shown to be a
model for the family, which she feared was threatened with
disintegration. Celine allowed herself to be interrogated
twice for hours and hours about her father and mother. Once
she was "under cross-examination for seven hours."

At 89, she continued to help with the writings, giving
depositions, rereading all the proofs. She carried out her
plan of erecting a statue of Therese. At eighty-nine, Celine
went up to the attic to explore trunks of family records. Her
parents' bodies were exhumed at this time. Celine and her
infirmarian gathered, sorted, washed with alcohol, and clas-
sified under a wax seal the dust and debris from the coffin,
"without removing anything except the bones." Literally,
she was at the end of her strength, but with the very peaceful
sense that her task as at last finished.[206]

I believe that women readers especially will be amused
by this paragraph about Celine in extreme old age:

"For some time, without anyone around her noticing
it, she had felt that she was aging terribly. She saw in
this a source of blessings. She showed more serenity
than in the past in putting up with changes. Speaking
of certain ornaments that she had long taken care of
and that the modern taste for simplification had set
aside, she said: 'I thank God for allowing me to see
this in my lifetime and enabling me to be lovingly detached from it.'

"The form of this world is passing away', she repeated in the face of certain traditions that had become outdated and at the sight of old customs pushed
to the background. Her whole impulse carried her toward heaven. The verse from the Apocalypse: 'Behold, I am coming soon. Yes, I am coming soon,"
thrilled her. The approaching denouement filled her

with great hope. 'It's not that I want to be delivered from suffering and work,' she explained, 'It's finally to be near my Jesus, whom I have loved for so long a time; near the Blessed Virgin, my dear Mother, and Saint Joseph; in order to know at last all the details of their life here on earth.'"[207]

Fr. Piat, her biographer, reports that Celine loved the following stanza from *Le Viellard* (the Old Man) by Msgr. Baunard:

"I am nearing a hundred, my day draws to a close;

It is more than evening, it is almost night.

But in front of me, rises in the east

The dawn of a more beautiful day. Welcome, welcome!

It is the white light of your face, O Christ,

Which in my sad heart awakens a great hope;

Come down, heavenly ray, appear, my Brother,

Jesus, it is time for us to see each other."[208]

At the end of her life she thought that God would just have to accept all her weaknesses — some were to insist on expressing her opinion when she disagreed about something. "Vibrant and warlike," she said she would always be. And even in the last years she loved Catholic scholarship.

These words written by Celine in her late eighties should give us plenty to think about:

"The other night I understood that it was suffering accepted with love that gave value to my life: Physical sufferings like those of martyrdom. Up until now I have suffered in all sorts of ways, in mind and in heart, suffered also from difficult and ponderous work, which Saint Paul enumerates in his list of tribulations. But what crowns life is personal suffering, like that of Job, afflicted in his own body. Saint Paul ended his very tormented life by the martyrdom of blood. Our Lord has said: 'Was it not necessary that

Christ should suffer and so enter into his glory?' Suffering in itself has no value; one has only to look at the demons and those damned. But accepted with loving abandonment to God, it is a divine seal put upon our life...It seemed to me that I saw it clearly, and I thanked God effusively for allowing me to pass through this crucible."[209]

And more ecstatically, something Celine wrote at fifty-seven about death:

"During my thanksgiving, I thought of death, as I usually do, and I said to myself that it was the greatest and most meritorious action of my life, an action I would perform only once. Then, I experienced an immense desire to accomplish this action as perfectly as possible, and I told myself that it would not be enough to die of love in an act of perfect love, but that I wanted it to be such a love that it breaks my bonds."[210]

As she was dying, Celine said that perhaps Little Therese wanted her to show the world that you can be little and simple even in extreme old age. "I am like a weary traveler who finally sees the doors to her father's house open before her."[211]

The Witness of Mother Teresa

Even though at this writing it is too early for the canonization process of Mother Teresa to have even begun, there is no question that she is considered to be a saint and that her words ring with an authenticity no one in our miserable, bloody century can dismiss.

Excerpts from her writings and narrations of others about her life come from several sources, as you will be able to see in the footnotes.[212] I am inserting in this chapter only thoughts that add to those already presented, for in editing the draft of my book it is obvious that repetition can blunt the force of ideas no matter how beautiful they may be.

"With Jesus our Savior, lamb led to the slaughter, and with the poor, we will accept cheerfully and in a spirit of faith all the opportunities he gives us of a greater gift: to share in the silence, loneliness, and agony of his Passion in our own life, due to humiliations, misunderstanding, false blame, rejections, failures, incapacities, corrections, temptations, lack of virtue, separation, sickness, old age, and death."[213]

(How easily I forget this basic Christian perspective! Of course, since we are destined for an eternity of happiness, if we open ourselves to God's way, we cannot rest in misery without longing for joy. However, we have to always remind ourselves that our greatest joy is in the hope of heaven, for on earth, Jesus never promised us freedom from the cross.)

"I never forgot the opportunity I had in visiting a home where they had all these old parents of sons and daughters who had just put them in an institution and forgotten them. I went there, and I saw in that home they had everything, beautiful things, but everybody was looking toward the door. And I did not see a single one with a smile on their face. And I turned to the Sister and I said, 'How is that? How is it that these people who have everything here, why are they all looking toward the door? Why are they not smiling?'

"I am so used to seeing smiles on our people; even the dying ones smile. She said, 'This happens nearly every day. They are expecting, they are hoping that a son or a daughter will come to visit them.' They are hurt because they are forgotten. And see — this is where love comes. That poverty comes right into our own home, even neglect of love. Maybe in our own family we have somebody who is feeling lonely, who is feeling sick, who is feeling worried, and these are difficult days for everybody. Are we there? Are we there to receive them?"[214]

(This famous narrative of Mother Teresa had a great impact on my life. My mother was in a beautiful residence for the aging, but she was deeply lonely. Since I had lots of conflict with my mother over a long period of time, I was always finding excuses not to visit. Listening to a tape with these words of Mother Teresa on it in her wonderful, powerful voice, I bowed my head and vowed to do all I could for my mother for the rest of her time on earth. Many results came from this breakthrough. In the last months of my mother's life I forced myself to take her into my home. Since I was working full-time with a long commute, it was absolutely clear that she needed an attendant. After some false starts the Lord sent a Philippino woman to tend my mother. It turned out this sweet compassionate woman had formerly worked with Mother Teresa's nuns in the care of the dying. She spent her time with my mother praying the rosary and singing Catholic hymns.)

"Suffering has to come because if you look at the cross, he has got his head bending down — he wants to kiss you — and he has both hands open wide — he wants to embrace you. He has his heart opened wide to receive you. Then when you feel miserable inside, look at the cross and you will know what is happening. Suffering, pain, sorrow, humiliation, feelings of lonelines, are nothing but the kiss of Jesus, a sign that you have come so close that he can kiss you."[215]

(Many of us who have spent more than half our lives in the post Vatican II Church have lost Mother Teresa's sense of the meaning of suffering. When we think of being Christian in a way that would emphasize joy more than suffering we can find ourselves in a place where our sufferings make no sense at all. Despair is soon to follow. Let us rush into the arms of Jesus when we feel the worst.)

Does that mean that we will never have joy again? That is not Mother Teresa's teaching. Read this:

"Remember that the Passion of Christ ends always in the joy of the resurrection of Christ, so when you feel in your own heart the suffering of Christ, remember the resurrection has to come, the joy of Easter has to dawn. Never let anything so fill you with sorrow as to make you forget the joy of Christ risen."[216]

"I must not attempt to control God's actions; I must not count the stages in the journey he would have me make. I must not desire a clear perception of my advance along the road, nor know precisely where I am on the way of holiness. I ask him to make a saint of me, yet I must leave to him the choice of that saintliness itself and still more the choice of the means which lead to it."[217]

(This above excerpt has a particular meaning for the aging. We are in the "end-game," and now it is even more absurd than formerly to imagine we can chart our own course. Suppose it turns out that precisely these joys and these sufferings I am experiencing because of being too old to be part of the party or the rat-race are the ones that will ready my soul for eternal happiness?)

"One day a man was brought in screaming and yelling. He didn't want to die. His backbone was broken in three places, and he had many terrible ulcers. His pain was intense. He didn't want to see the Sisters. He didn't want to die. He was given morphine and love in generous doses, and he was told of the sufferings of One who loved him very much. Gradually he began to listen and to accept love. On his last day, he refused the morphine because he wanted to be united to the One who saved him."[218]

One day a co-worker sent a message to Mother Teresa that she would not be able to accompany her because she had a fever. "Mother Teresa remarked, 'I also have a fever, but it is better to burn in this world than in the next.'"[219]

(As we age, very often we feel that we can do no more we feel so terrible. The above anecdote challenges us to do the most we can even when we don't feel good at all. If I can't do much, why not do whatever I can still do that helps people vs. sitting home moaning?)

This story is especially important for those who really can't do anything outside their homes:

"Jacqueline (de Decker) wanted to work with her (Mother), but before she could she had to return to Belgium for medical treatment. During her stay in Belgium, she developed a paralysis that affected an arm, an eye, and a leg. Then followed 20 operations on her spine. Her chances of returning to work with Mother Teresa in India were negligible. She wrote to Mother Teresa, who realized the practical difficulties of Jacqueline working with the poorest of the poor, but that didn't mean that Mother Teresa thought that Jacqueline had nothing to offer. She suggested that, from her home in Belgium, Jacqueline could support the work that was being done in India through her own suffering and her prayers. And so was born the Sick and Suffering Co-Workers of Mother Teresa, who link themselves to the suffering of others through prayer and their own pain."[220]

Some people think that the Catholic Church doesn't allow for leadership of women. An answer surely lies in the beauty of an old nun in her 80's giving a speech like this to the 1994 Synod of Bishops in Rome:

"Our lives must be to thirst after Jesus. This aim of the Missionaries of Charity is to quench the thirst of Jesus on the Cross for the love of souls by working for the salvation and sanctification of the poorest of the poor...

"Our life as religious, and especially as women, must be to thirst with Jesus by taking upon ourselves the thirst of our people and of all those entrusted to our care...We must remember that Jesus fully became man and thirsts for our love, just as we thirst for each other's love...

"Religious women by their vows of chastity, poverty and obedience must bring people, thirsting for love, to

Jesus...Our vow of chastity liberates us totally to contemplate God and to give wholehearted and free service to all men. Our vow of poverty is our dowry which allows us to be married to Christ who is poor and a friend of the poor. Through our vow of obedience, we listen to God's word spoken through His creatures and we obey joyfully as did Our Lady...Because of the desire to enter the mystery of Jesus in the Eucharist, the Missionaries of Charity have four hours of prayer every day, including a daily adoration of one hour before the Blessed Sacrament.

"We pray daily after receiving Jesus in Holy Communion, the prayer 'Radiating Christ.' In our chapels, we put a transparent veil on the tabernacle to remind us we must become so transparent, that people only see Jesus through us and we will see Jesus in them...

"I look to the Blessed Virgin Mary as the one I must follow as a religious, especially as a woman who is a religious. Mary was the first consecrated woman...Let us pray daily to Mary our Mother and our Confidence: 'Mary, Our Mother, give us your heart so beautiful, so pure, so immaculate, so full of love and humility that we may be able to receive Jesus in the Bread of Life, love Him as you loved Him and serve Him in the distressing disguise of the poor.'"

And here is a letter to the co-workers in 1992 by a male follower of Mother Teresa, Brother Andrew, about the greatness of her influence at the age of eighty-two:

"It's approaching 30 years since I have known and worked closely with Mother Teresa. The old principle of familiarity leading to taking wonderful things for granted intrudes everywhere. So it was good to meet her again on a recent visit to Calcutta after four years.

"She has aged, she has been sick, she looks frail, her voice is weaker. But to hear her tell a little of what she is involved in is to catch a tiny glimpse of a woman in our times of extraordinary influence.

"In scarcely an hour, you hear that she has opened ten communities in Russia with her sisters — and more are coming; fifteen girls in Albania have joined her congregation — some of them having to be baptized because of the strict repression for years. Postulants, too, come in Rumania and Hungary.

"She has seven convents opened in Cuba in the last few years, and keeps personal contact with Fidel Castro. You pick up a mutual respect between the two, while they retain their own very different faiths.

"She tells of a State governor in America phoning to ask her what he should do about the final decision he has to make about the death penalty for a convicted murderer. Her words to him: "Do what Jesus would do." A week later the news is released that it is life imprisonment.

"The law in Albania had worship as a capital offense. She was asked by the president to open six churches that had been used for secular purposes. And she adds in that impish way: 'And I opened a mosque for the Muslims.' — after helping with her sisters to sweep and clean it. Needless to say, Muslim-Christian relations in the new Albania are off to a good start.

"She has recently been to Iraq at the invitation of Sadam Hussein, and has sisters there caring for the orphans of war and the many maimed children — somehow getting supplies past sanctions, embargoes, or whatever.

"She tells of two elected politicians from American who, on the last day of a visit to India, said they would like to meet the poor. She put them to work in the home for the dying destitute. They cleaned, washed, shaved men, they fed people who couldn't hold a spoon. They went almost directly to the airport some hours later, and she received a letter thanking her: 'It has changed my life. I'll never be the same again.'

"Doctors and medical staff in Russia have seen her sisters doing the simple cleaning and loving in their hospital.

'What we do here,' wrote a young Indian sister, 'is very simple. We clean the toilets and smile at the patients.' And the director says the atmosphere of the whole hospital has changed.

"The next day she was moving off to Cambodia to try to iron out difficulties with the government over visas for her sisters, and greater freedom to work for the poorest.

"With all this she had spent hours the day before at the bedside of a young sister seriously injured by a careening truck as she walked on the street."

A rich reflection on the woman lies behind each of these stories that can easily be missed:

"The State Chief Minister, or Premier, of West Bengal is a life-long, strong, still-practicing Communist at the head of a Communist State government. He and Mother Teresa have known and respected each other for years. With the limited social welfare resources of his government, a large group of women who had been kidnaped or trapped into prostitution were kept in prison because there was no other possibility.

"The Chief Minister, Jyoti Basu, phoned Mother Teresa to take them, saying they shouldn't be in a jail. She took forty. He made state land available, and she has built a place for these and more. The ready co-operation between Christian nun and committed communist around the desperate, urgent plight of helpless victims is fertile ground for social concern, liberation and evangelization..."

As she leaves, the practical woman in her notices the bananas growing richly in the Brothers' garden and she asks, "What do you do with these bananas?" She is satisfied to hear that they are shared with the poor.

The following passages have to do with Mother Teresa's life after her resignation as head of the Missionaries of Charity when she was too old and ill to continue in that post. Still, she vowed that she would do whatever she could until her last breath.

In a letter to the co-workers in 1996, Mother Teresa says that "Jesus does not make mistakes," so she must accept His will in her "retirement." Mother Teresa died at the age of eighty-seven.

From a November, 1997 letter from Mother Nirmala who took over for Mother Teresa: Mother Teresa left (as of her death, 9/5/97) 3803 professed sisters, 292 postulants and 466 novices, a total of 585 houses in 120 countries (18 of which she helped to open in the year before her death). In the year before her death, she was made an honorary citizen of Rome and given an Italian Diplomatic passport; honorary US citizenship; the "Gold Medal" — the highest award given by the Albanian government; in India — the "HOPE Unity Award" and in June, 1997 the Congressional Medal of Honor given by the US government. In the year before she died, Shishyu Bhavan in Calcutta admitted 329 babies of whom 61 were adopted in India and 179 abroad. Also — 130 slum schools; sewing, typing and English classes; visiting families (approx. 190,000), shut-ins, hospitals, nursing homes and prisons; 213 homes for abandoned, malnourished and handicapped children, 250 for sick and dying destitutes, 19 for AIDS sufferers, 14 leprosy homes, night shelters, mobile clinics; day creches, homes for unwed mothers, alcohol and drug dependents; Sunday school and other religious instruction. The Brothers numbering 366 professed and 47 novices in 68 houses run 37 dispensaries, 22 slum schools, homes for dying destitutes, TB, cancer, leprosy and disabled, operate relief centers and centers for youth and street children — built 82 houses for leprosy patients and orphans in 1997. The Missionaries of Charity priests had 4 houses in 1997 — Tijuana, Mexico City, Rome and Calcutta. Then there are contemplative brothers — 4 houses: 2 in Albania, 1 in Rome and 1 in Delhi. Contemplative sisters — 18 houses.

A prayer to the saints to intercede for us:

Shame fills my heart, my Jesus, when I think of the attitude of the saints to the crosses of aging. The joy of aging for the saints was ever the knowledge that they were getting closer to you. May all the saints, those who died young and those who died old, pray for us that the last part of our lives may be the best.

FOR PERSONAL REFLECTION AND GROUP SHARING:
1. What images or lines from the lives of the aging saints do you want to remember?
2. Are there any saints who died in old age I didn't mention who you want to think about, write about, or share about in your group?

At the Gates of Eternity

If you are like me, you may have been so overwhelmed by the witness of the saints that you wonder what could possibly come next. I understand. But, but, but! If I had ended this book with the accomplishments of Mother Teresa, pretty soon after closing the book you would be saying: "But, but, but...what if I'm not a saint? What about my doubts? What about my fears? Aren't we going to read anything for ordinary non-saints like me who still wonder: is eternal life for real? What does the Church teach anyhow about things other than heaven, such as purgatory and hell? How should I pray to be sure I'm going to a good place?"

In his booklet *Jaws of Death: Gates of Heaven*, [221] the great philosopher and spiritual writer of our time, Dietrich Von Hildebrand, explains that even for those with ardent faith in the promises of Christ, the reality of death can be a cause of horror. To think that the body that has been intimately joined to the soul for so many years is to perish is a formidable and frightening thought. To consider that the most beloved persons I have known as present to me in their bodies will no longer be accessible to me on this earth has to be one of the worst sources of misery. It is not by nature, but by grace that we are able to endure the thought of our own death and that of loved ones. If you yourself, or someone dear to you, is overwhelmed by fear of death, Christian writings which skip over the phase of horror at death will usually not be helpful. Instead, it would be good to get hold of Von Hildebrand's booklet showing how hope in Christ follows a thorough description of how terrible the reality of death truly is.

My little book *Victory Over Death*[222] can serve another purpose. This meditative book includes a series of reflections about the immortality of the soul, including philosophical proofs, and ways to think of eternity that will help someone fearing death to see it precisely as a gateway to heaven.

In this chapter of *Seeking Christ in the Crosses and Joys of Aging*, however, I want to draw your attention instead to the authoritative teachings of the Church and the writings of saints and other holy people. At the end I will provide rites and tried and true prayers that can help us in the most important transition after conception we will ever have to make!

Church Teaching about Our Transition to Eternity
(As you read you might circle passages you would like to return to in the future.)

> *Be gracious to me, O Lord, for I am in distress;*
> *my eye is wasted from grief,*
> *my soul and my body also.*
> *For my life is spent with sorrow*
> *and my years with sighing;*
> *my strength fails because of my misery;*
> *and my bones waste away...*
> *Be strong, and let your heart take courage,*
> *all you who wait for the Lord!"* (Psalm 31, 9-10, 24)

"Truly no man can ransom himself,
or give to God the price of his life,
for the ransom of his life is costly, and can never suffice,
that he should continue to live on for ever,
and never see the Pit...
But God will ransom my soul from
the power of Sheol,
for he will receive me." (Psalm 49: 7-9, 15)
"He will swallow up death for ever, and the Lord God will wipe
away tears
from all faces..." (Isaiah 25:08)
"Where are your plagues, O death!
Where is your sting, O nether world!" (Hosea 13:14)
"But if Christ is in you, although your bodies are dead because
of sin,
your spirits are alive because of righteousness.
If the Spirit of him who raised Jesus from the dead dwells in you,
he who raised Christ Jesus from the dead will give life to your
mortal
bodies also through his Spirit which dwells in you." (Romans 8:
10-11)
"How can some of you say that there is no resurrection of the
dead?
But if there is no resurrection of the dead, then Christ has not
been raised; if Christ
has not been raised, then our preaching is in vain and your faith
is in vain...
But in fact Christ has been raised from the dead, the first fruits
of those who
have fallen asleep." (1 Corinthians 15:12-14)
"I long to be freed from this life and to be with Christ."
(Philippians 1:23)

As you can see from the Scriptures given above in the Old and New Testament, there are references to a life beyond the present one on earth. The Church's teachings about life after death have always been clearly stated. Yet as we approach the gates of eternity many of us need a kind of "refresher course." Sometimes it is because the promises seem too good to be true. Sometimes it is because we have been so preoccupied with worldly affairs that we have not sufficiently pondered the truths expressed weekly in the Creed.

Let's not guess about this all important topic. In contemporary language, the *Catechism of the Catholic Church*[223], released in 1994, summarizes the perennial teachings of our Church for all to read. (Numbers in this text are from paragraphs in this Catechism.)

"We firmly believe, and hence we hope that, just as Christ is truly risen from the dead and lives forever, so after death the righteous will live forever with the risen Christ and he will raise them up on the last day." (#989) This resurrection will include the body in a new form.

Many passages from Scripture concern the reality of everlasting life, such as 2 Maccabees 7; John 6: 39-40; Romans 8:11; 1 Thessalonians 4:16.

The authors of the Catechism explain that God gradually revealed the nature of eternal life to His people. (#992) We are to participate in the resurrection of Christ's body through living in Him while on earth. In death the soul is separated from the decaying body. It is immediately present to God for judgement. There is no reincarnation. On the last day, at the end of this world, the body will be resurrected and rejoin the soul. (#997, #1013)

Many of the words of Jesus speak about reward and punishment. (See #1021)

"Those who die in God's grace and friendship and are perfectly purified live forever with Christ. They are like God forever, for they 'see him as he his,' face to face." (#1023) They dwell in communion with the Blessed Trinity, the Virgin Mary, the angels, and all the blessed. They enjoy the beatific vision and experience perfect happiness.

"All who die in God's grace and friendship, but still imperfectly purified, are indeed assured of their eternal salvation; but after death they undergo purification, so as to achieve the holiness necessary to enter the joy of heaven." (#1030) This period is called Purgatory. The Church has always practiced prayer for the dead, which would be needless if those who died went to either heaven or hell with no state in between needing the help of grace. (See #1031-1032)

"We cannot be united with God unless we freely choose to love him. But we cannot love God if we sin gravely against him, against our neighbor or against ourselves: 'He who does not love remains in death. Anyone who hates his brother is a murderer, and you know that no murderer has eternal life abiding in him.' (1 Jn 3:14-15) Our Lord warns us that we shall be separated from him if we fail to meet the serious needs of the poor and the little ones who are his brethren. (Cf. Mt. 25:31-46) To die in mortal sin without repenting and accepting God's merciful love means remaining separated from him for ever by our own free choice. This state of definitive self-exclusion from communion with God and the blessed is called 'hell.'"(#1033)

At the Last Judgment, as depicted in Scripture, all will come to be judged. (See #1038-1041) The universe itself will be renewed as a new heaven and a new earth. (Revelations 21:1) All tears will be wiped away and the visible world will be restored to the state it was in Paradise. (#1047)

Beautiful as is this panorama of fulfillment in the world to come, most Christians have felt the need for greater illumination about the exact nature of our heavenly state. For this reason I am including here a few reflections from the doctors of the Church, Augustine and Aquinas, for your edification:

Here is a commentary on Scripture by the greatest Father of the Church, St. Augustine:

"'We shall be like Him, for we shall see Him as He is.' ...The entire life of a good Christian is in fact an exercise of

holy desire. You do not see what you long for, but that very act of desiring prepares you, so that when He comes you may see and be utterly satisfied.

"Suppose you are going to fill some holder or container, and you know you will be given a large amount. Then you set about stretching your sack or wineskin or whatever it is. Why? Because you know the quantity you will have to put in it and your eyes tell you there is not enough room. By stretching it, therefore, you increase the capacity of the sack, and this is how God deals with us. Simply by making us wait He increases our desire, which in turn enlarges the capacity of our soul, making it able to receive what is to be given to us.

"So, my brethren, let us continue to desire, for we shall be filled – (like St. Paul) *'forgetting what lies behind, and stretching forward to what lies ahead, I press on toward the prize to which I am called in the life above.'"*[224]

What did the greatest Doctor of the Church, St. Thomas Aquinas, teach about life after death? Hundreds of pages of his writings are devoted to this topic.[225] Here I can only summarize.

On a purely philosophical plane, Thomas was interested in showing that the soul by its very nature is immaterial, hence not subject to death simply because the material body dies. The gist of his argument is that an immaterial entity, not having physical parts, does not break up. How do we know that the human soul is immaterial? As an entity acts, so it is. The human soul which includes our mental capacities is able to know immaterial entities such as concepts and universal truths. A way I explain this in philosophy classes is this: How much more does the thought "love" weigh than the thought "toenail"? Obviously, it's a stupid question because a concept doesn't weigh anything at all. It just exists in the mind in an immaterial way. If the mind can know immaterial entities, then it itself must be immaterial. We don't really believe that one person has half a soul and another a quarter of a soul. The soul is simply a spiritual reality equally present in any human being in terms of its basic reality. So, if the soul is immaterial, as Thomas shows, (see Question 75 of the *Summa Theologica*) then it doesn't fall into material parts when the body dies. It lives on.

Here is a summary of one of Aquinas' teachings on the glorified body in heaven:

Referring to the words of St. Paul: "What is sown in the earth is subject to decay, what rises is incorruptible. What is sown is ignoble, what rises is glorious. Weakness is sown, strength rises up! A natural body is put down and a spiritual body comes up!" (1 Corinthians 15:42-44)

St. Thomas Aquinas identifies four properties of the glorified body:

Impassibility — Freedom from suffering physical evils: death, sorrow, illness, etc.

Subtlety — A power to penetrate (pass through) material objects.

Agility — A power to move easily and quickly, not weighed down.

Clarity — Full of splendor, radiance and brilliance.

"Thus in the glorified body the glory of the soul will be known, even as through a crystal is known the color of a body contained in a crystal vessel."[226]

Many wonder how the body in heaven can be "roaming about," meeting people and loving transfigured nature if the soul is transfixed in the beatific vision of God. Thomas insists that it is possible in heaven to simultaneously be enraptured in God, yet relate to other beings in the resurrected body.

Readers interested in further knowledge about what theologians have said about eternal life might want to read Peter Kreeft's fine popular volume entitled *All You Wanted to Know about Heaven*.[227]

Spiritual Reflections

Besides high theology, I get a lot of help from more informal spiritual reflections concerning our transition to eternal life. Before moving to the writings of saints and holy people, I would like to share with you a little poem I wrote about my mother as she neared her death in 1987:

Tired from
the long
journey
upstream
her soul
treads water;
scans the
dark night
for what
is to come.
We who
would be lighthouses
seem but
flickering
vigil candles
on the remote shore.
Into Thy hands
we commend
her spirit.
Our Lady
Star of the Sea
guide her home.

The image of the seafarer is good for me. I am also fond of the traditional analogy of death to a deep sleep in which one emigrates from this world, maybe in the form of an old servant whose work is accomplished and who then finally leaves the house where she has worked so long. Also the idea of shuffling off the body like a snake-skin has an appeal. Of course, the cocoon to butterfly image has been helpful to many pondering the mystery of death. I think of this transformation from something relatively ugly and confined to something beautiful and free as meaning that we have to accept being slowly reduced to next to nothing so that, pride totally crushed, all we will have left is Jesus. Once I thought I heard Jesus say in my heart about death, "All that will be left then will be your heart and Mine."

Colloquial expressions for death can conceal insights into the real beliefs of the person using them. It has got to make a difference is someone says about a dead man, "He's pushing up daisies," or "He went to Jesus." Or how about the phrase, "He got away from us!"

Here are some of my favorite sayings about death from the saints. They are all to be found in one chapter of my book *Quotable Saints*[228].

St. Cyril of Jerusalem — "The root of all good works is the hope of the resurrection; for the expectation of the reward [moves] the soul to good works."

St. Cyprian — "For it is for him to fear death who is not willing to go to Christ."

St. Anthony the Great — "As the body must be born after completing its development in the womb, so a soul, when it has reached the limit of life in the body allotted it by God, must leave the body."

St. Hippolytus — "We shall enter the kingdom of heaven, because while we lived on earth we acknowledged heaven's king."

St. Ambrose — "To the good man to die is gain. The foolish fear death as the greatest of evils. The wise desire it as a rest after labors and the end of ills."

St. Augustine — "O what consequence is it what kind of death puts an end to life, since he who has died once is not forced to go through the same ordeal a second time...The bodies of the saints will therefore rise again free from every defect, from every deformity, as well as from every corruption, encumbrance, or hindrance. In this respect their freedom of action will be as complete as their happiness."

St. Anthony the Great — "Life is union and junction of mind [spirit], soul and body; death is the disruption of their union; God preserve it all even after this disruption."

St. Peter Chrysologus — "A gentle maiden [Mary], having lodged a God in her womb, asks as its price, peace for the world, salvation for those who are lost, and life for the dead."

St. Clotilda — (On the death of her baby): "I give thanks to Almighty God that He has not considered me unworthy to be the mother of a child admitted into the celestial kingdom. Having quitted the world in the white robe of his innocence, he will rejoice in the presence of God through all eternity."

St. Bernard — "I can never lose one whom I have loved unto the end; one to whom my soul cleaves so firmly that it can never be separated does not go away but only goes before. Be mindful of me when you come to where I shall follow you."

These next quotations from St. Bernard come from a newly printed book of his letters to various friends. They touch my heart by the combination of such total faith in the reality of eternal life combined with human love.[229]

"Be mindful of me when you come to where I shall follow you, so that I may be permitted soon to come after you...In the meantime be sure that I shall never lose the dear memory of you, although to my sorrow I lose your dear presence."[230]

"Pitiful, pitiful beyond measure, are those who spend their lives enjoying the good things of the world, so that 'full of ease their life passes and they go down at last without a struggle to the grave. For they cannot take all with them when they die...Think of this, dearest friend, let it be your daily meditation, emblazon it on your heart, and never let it slip from your memory. Farewell."[231]

"I indeed love your body, but I love more your soul. Just as I do not love my own body except for the sake of my soul, so too is my love for you...Take away the soul and what is left of the body, except what can be said of every human body: 'Dust thou are and to dust thou shalt return'? The soul still lives after it has been released form the body, unless it is so loaded with sin that, when the body returns to the earth from which it was taken, the soul cannot, in the words of Scripture, 'return to God who gave it.' It is not right to love equally what moves and what is moved, what rules and what is ruled, what is of the earth earthy and what has come from above signed with the image of a higher nature...Why do you still keep the company of men with whose outlook you have no sympathy?...Do you cling only to the Lord...If he is good to those that seek him, how much more so is he to those that find him!"[232]

We need before we die to "scrape off the filth of secular life...to shake off the dust of the world."[233]

"What room can there be in me for pleasure when suffering claims me completely for her own? The only sort of pleasure I have is in eating nothing. So that suffering may never be absent from me, even sleep has left me...My feet and legs are swollen as though I had dropsy. But in the midst of all this, so as to conceal nothing from an anxious friend, according to the inward man I have a ready spirit in a weak body. Pray our Savior, who wills not the death of a sinner, that he will not put off my timely departure, but that he may watch over me in passing. Support, I beg you, with your prayers a poor wretch destitute of all virtue, so that the enemy who lies in wait for me may find no place where he can grip me with his teeth and wound me. I have written this with my own hand so that when you see the familiar writing you may recognize how well I love you."[234]

Returning to my excerpts in my book *Quotable Saints*[235]:

St. Herman of Reichenau — "The whole of this present world has become mean and wearisome, and on the other hand the world to come has become so unspeakably desirable and dear that I hold all these passing things as light as thistledown. I am tired of 'living.'"

St. Francis of Assisi — "Blessed be God for our sister, the death of the body."

St. Gertrude the Great — (Jesus is said to have told Gertrude) "My heaven would not be complete without you."

Blessed Margaret Colonna — "I thank thee, dear Lord, for having permitted my body to become weak and infirm, so that I could more freely return my soul to Thee."

Blessed Julian of Norwich — "My understanding was lifted up into heaven, where I saw our Lord like a lord in his own house who has called all his valued servants and friends to a solemn feast...and [Christ] filled [the house] with joy and mirth. He himself endlessly gladdened and solaced his valued friends...with the marvelous melody of endless love in his own fair blessed face. This glorious countenance of the godhead completely fills all heaven with joy and bliss...God showed three degrees of bliss that every soul that has willingly served god...shall have in heaven. The first is the gratitude...he shall receive from our Lord God...the second is that all the blessed creatures who are in heaven shall see the glorious thanking...the third...is that it shall last forever."

St. Catherine of Siena — "The martyrs desired death, not to fly labor, but to attain their goal. And why do they not fear death, from which man naturally shrinks? Because they had vanquished the natural love of their own bodies by divine and supernatural love."

St. Teresa of Avila — "Over my spirit flash and float in divine radiancy the bright and glorious visions of the world to which I go."

Blessed Junipero Serra — "Life is uncertain and, in fact, may be very brief. If we compare it with eternity, [we] will clearly realize that it cannot be but more than an instant. A happy death of all the things of life is our principal concern. For if we attain that, it matters little if we lose all the rest. But if we do not attain that, nothing else will be of any value."

Blessed Henry Morse — (about to be martyred) — "Come, my sweetest Jesus, that I may now be inseparably united to thee in time and eternity: welcome ropes, hurdles, gibbets, knives and butchery, welcome for the love of Jesus, my savior."

St. Lugartha Lee Yu-Hye (Korean martyr) — "I have no further desire to live and only think of giving my life to God."

St. Elizabeth Seton — "...Of that house in which the soul wavers between its future and its present home, mine is transported at even the probability [of death] for the bonds that hold it have scarcely strength to restrain it...and if reason and the best affections of this world did not withhold and draw back with more than common force its flying propensities, I should have renounced every other desire and aim long ago."

St. Theophane Venard — "I shall be beheaded. Within a few short hours my soul will quite this earth, exile over, and battle won. I shall mount upwards and enter into our true home. There among God's elect I shall gaze upon what eye of man cannot imagine, hear undreamed of harmonies, enjoy a happiness the heart cannot comprehend."

St. Dominic Savio — (On his deathbed) "What a beautiful thing I see."

St. Joseph Mukasa Balikuddembe — (On his way to martyrdom) "Why should you bind me? From whom should I escape? From God?"

Blessed Rafka al-Rayes — "I am not afraid. I have been waiting for my Lord for a long time. He is the one who has made me love death and now my one desire is to go and be with Him"

St. Gemma Galgani — "Jesus, destroy this chain of a body, for I shall never be content till my soul can fly to you. When shall I be completely blessed in you?"

Venerable Charles de Foucauld — "Remember that you ought to die as a martyr, stripped of everything, stretched naked on the ground, unrecognizable, covered with wounds and blood, killed violently and painfully — and desire that it be today...Think often of death, so as to prepare for it and appraise things at their true value."

Venerable Thecla Merlo — "There are difficulties, sufferings, and worries...But one beautiful day it will be all over, and we will find ourselves all united in Heaven with the Blessed Trinity, with Mary most holy, with our dear ones and with the Sisters who have gone before us. This is our joy and our comfort. Courage!"

Venerable Jose Escriva — "You, if you are an apostle, will not have to die. You will move to a new house: that's all."

Having, I hope, delighted you with these short passages, I still want to give you just a little more for this chapter on "At The Gates of Eternity" from some of the spiritual writers you have met in earlier chapters:

Blythe is back! Originally, I picked out this British sociologist to read just to get a sense of what wisdom I might find in the world. Imagine my amazed delight to find that by the end of his long book, he is presenting a truly Christian perspective on aging!

Some examples:

"Young people often say, 'Would you like to be young again?' And don't really like it when you say no. I soften the blow. I say, 'Just think of all the years I should have been done out of heaven!' Though that doesn't please them either. When you are young, you think it is better to be young than in heaven. It was dreadful for many to be old in my boyhood. For working people there was still the fear of the workhouse....

"On the day of my wife's death her face was very stricken and it was hard to look at. She had double pneumonia after an operation. Her change panicked me and I called people and nurses and doctors. She couldn't communicate, but needed to. And she suddenly sat up, smiled, put our her arms and died. Her last words were a gesture. I thought I was seeing things when I saw her face. Even her hair glowed. When I looked in to see my lady after her death, she had the face of a girl. That is how we enter the presence of Christ — at our best. In full revelation."[236]

This is a passage from an interview Blythe did with an aging religious monk:

"One can hardly expect to ask for pity or show regret simply because one is within sight of home. Death is not their great worry, and they are remarkably buoyant when confronted by geriatric diseases. What disturbs them most about age is the decay of spiritual passion. Prayer is not what it was...As one of them said, so often having nothing to offer, he offers Nothing. For increasing stretches of time, it is all he has now, and he offers his all — Nothing. Cowper summed it up when he wrote of the toil 'Of dropping buckets into empty wells,/ And growing old in drawing nothing up."[237]

But then to this troubling quotation, Blythe adds this lovely one from Richard Crowley in *Treasures of Hope:*

"This is no home, this is but a lodging...I must begin to long for home. I seem almost asleep, but my heart is awake. It does not think, or plan or labor to remember, but it loves; it is withdrawn from the surface of life to the center...My God, I would not die as the unconscious things, the frozen sparrow under the hedge, the dead leaf whirled away before the night wind."[238]

Father George Congreve of the order where Blythe was doing his research,

"...describes the thinning of the scene of life by loss of objects and interests, and of personal littleness being no longer chilling. His horror of shriveling up as inconsequentially as a leaf passes away; he sees 'that small faculty of love, our personality itself, begins to grow as it begins to contemplate the infinite Love,' and he breathes again as 'the abyss of Deity is no longer a fearful solitude and a desert...'"[239]

Here are some words from a Father Stephen, seventy-nine, which echo the counsel of Johnson, the expert on spirituality of aging, quoted in a former section:

"It is non-stop the dying of friends and acquaintances, when you are eighty...What does it mean not to be able to do things? Everybody screams — and I include myself — 'I can't do this and I can't do that!' And 'I used to do this and I used to do that' and 'Baaah!' The lesson to be learnt is to understand the promotion from plum-easy doing to the surprisingly difficult non-activity of just *being*. Be patient, be gentle, be *nothing*. Somebody said that the real vocation of old age was to give out love. So no more doing, but being. I told an old lady in a home this and she said, 'What a lot of rot. Never heard such a lot of rot!' But within a fortnight she'd begun to get the hang of it, and it made all the difference to her."[240]

Another monk who was in healing says that this ministry,

"...gives you a sensible interest in your old age. It stops that petering-out feeling. It even makes you care for your body because as the vehicle of your personality, you know you will be recognized by it on the next plane. I find my body very pleasant still; it's done me proud. It's quite nice still, if I say it myself. It all works. It reminds me of my earthly humanity, which I've so enjoyed."[241]

Here's a woman's point of view from an interview with a clergyman's widow who doesn't want presents because she's trying to get rid of things. She is tidying-up for when she goes,

"...so I'll be as little a nuisance as possible when the time comes. I dread having a stroke, because that is the most ghastly nuisance which will go on for months and months, and when I finally manage to go, my daily woman will say, 'Oh, what a nuisance she was, poor thing!'

"Except she won't because she is so good. Come to think of it, I could afford to be a bit of a nuisance with her. She wouldn't even notice it, I daresay. She has become my closest and most trusted friend now. She lets me rely on her, and anyone who will let you do that is worth their weight in gold. And the woman who does my shopping would come to me at once, if I needed her. I see them both as part of the goodness of God, you know...

"I don't dread being dead. My heavenly Father has looked after me from the cradle, and he won't stop at the grave. Through all my life he has taken care of me. Even if I just went out like a candle, what is there to dread?"[242]

A 90 year old English lady asks: "Don't you realize what death is? It is a lovely mist which takes us away." She had a near death experience when she was a young wife and mother:

"I, the real me, was alert and waiting to hop out of my body at any minute. And I could feel this mist coming towards me, a sort of swirling bank of marvelous love, love such as you'd never guess it in this world. And I could hear myself saying, 'Oh, take me, take me. Quick — take me!' And the mist started to go back slowly and it was most disappointing, and I came back to life...I believe that we are more alive...It's uncanny when you are old, the space and the silence which are left by all the people who used to be in your life. Believe me, there is nothing of the least importance left on this side when you get to my age. So, in other words, nearer, nearer, nearer God."[243]

Maybe out of envy of Ronald Blythe interviewing all these people and coming up with such wonderful gems, I decided to question a very spiritual pastor in a nearby parish in Arizona. Father James Kelly had just survived a sixth by-pass heart surgery. I wondered what his thoughts were about coming closer to the gates of eternity. Here are some of Fr. James Kelly's observations:

"Death is a good thing, a blessing, especially when one is terribly sick...Don't wait to pray in the hospital if you are very sick. Pray now, not when you are close to death; not when you are practically unconscious...When I came out of surgery I was very calm and tranquil. I never felt angry...I prayed for death many times in my life as did Moses, Elijah, Tobit, Jonas, Job. Most of the mystics hated life because of all the suffering and sin in it...But the essence of life is the acceptance of suffering with patience and resignation.

"Life gets harder as you age. Beginnings are the best...youth itself (even though growing up poor with nine children in a tiny place in 1934) and then early years of the priesthood. The young have high goals and ideals and are more positive about life...Still, I am a better priest because I have had such a hard life. Yet I am happiest now even though not the most productive...I still like to say Mass and take joy in my prayer-life. Adding up all the aspects of Mass and prayer I spend about five hours a day in prayer...I have more peace and joy inside because so much is behind me and I don't have that far to go...Before I die I wish I could see God come back into society again."

Just before I started writing this book my revered spiritual director, Fr. Luke Zimmer, died of cancer. Some of Fr. Luke's thoughts as he was suffering from that disease, as chronicled in his updated autobiography[244] could help some-one deal with the same kind of pain:

Here are some excerpts:

"I was hoping that people would not pray for (a miracle

for me, although) praying for a miracle is quite natural. But, most (of the time) a person does not need to be living to (do the will of) God. Rather, a person can carry out God's will (from heaven.) And I believe that this is my time to go Home because there is a time for everything, especially when it comes to fulfilling God's plan.

"In reference to my pancreatic cancer, God's Will must be done and a person does not have to use extraordinary means to prolong life. Rather, a person must use reasonable means so that nature can take its course. Only in using natural means is there real dignity in death, especially when there is not possibility of getting well. In other words, true dignity is not suicide or assisted suicide because God is the author of life and not man. God is the One Who calls us Home. Therefore, we must wait on God and accept all sufferings no matter what they may be. However, when there is hope of being cured, a person needs to use proper means to be healed.

"Presently, I don't feel any pain. Although I have lost quite a bit of weight through this whole ordeal. But now, I am starting to level off and I am regaining my strength. However, I know this strength will not last long because eventually I will lose some more weight and go through some suffering. Yet, I'm willing to do whatever God wants.

"Pancreatic cancer is called the silent killer. The cancer grows silently within a person. If a person is lucky enough and the doctors discover the cancer before it has progressed too far, it is possible to treat the cancer. However, after discovering the cancer after a particular stage, there is nothing that can be done..."

Fr. Luke included this poem written for him on his deathbed by a friend:

In His Presence
Bright yellow sun
ball, red encircling, sitting

together on
the western horizon.
Corn,
no longer the green
of August,
but dry
and you would think
fragile,
holds itself erect
in the field,
as does the man
faded now
and close to the end.
Life funnels into
the unknown
for infinitely less than
the blink of
an eye, is made
whole again
in His presence.

M. Ptacek

More of Fr. Luke's Meditations:

"I am very grateful to God because He has given me this time to prepare for eternal life. As a person comes closer to death, the more there is a need to let go of all that is earthly and to ponder on the real values of life. A person needs to let go and let God as well as to die more to self and become more like God each day. This is a great gift and opportunity. When a person lives for eternal life, he or she never needs to fear death...

"When I found out that I had terminal cancer, I wanted to contact Sr. Belane so that she would know about my cancer and pray for me. When we finally got in contact, she told me that she too had cancer and that she had been in the hospital for three weeks. Sr. Belane told me in 1946 that would join the Congregation of the Sacred Heart and that my religious name would be Luke. Ever since then, she has been praying for my priesthood and my ministry. She is ninety-two years old and we have remained very close over the years. In fact, I always remember her during Mass so that she would be blessed and benefit for everything she has ever done for me."

To turn to the insights of another spiritual writer familiar to you, Henri Nouwen, I had always wondered why this brilliant counselor, speaker, and writer was so interested in the elderly. This description of his grandmother's old age and death helped me understand:

"When I think of her I do not feel sad or depressed — rather a warm smile dawns on the horizons of my thoughts. I see her beautiful white hair and her small tender face which felt so soft every time she kissed me. Sitting in her easy chair, she listened with great attention to all the stories I had to tell about my father and mother, my brothers and sister, my studies and ordination, my plans and my hopes. And I knew for sure she was always on my side.

"When I complained about my teachers, she made me feel that I was right. When I talked about the long trips I had to make, she usually said: 'O poor boy.' When I told her how terribly busy I was, she was ready to become angry at anyone who could possibly be blamed. Whatever I said, she would always take it seriously.

"And although she seldom talked about her long past of eighty years, I saw in her eyes the slow life on a small Dutch farm. I saw the man she met and lived with for forty-five years, and their eleven children. I saw how she taught my father to walk, talk, and go his own way. I saw her endless, frightening asthmatic attacks. I saw her behind the window, looking at the hearse parked in front of the house, provoking a last memory of her husband being carried to his grave.

saw her knitting and knitting and knitting
ong scarves for me and all her grandchil-
n front of me with the rosary in her hands,
o nice that you anointed me, that was very
I am ready to go.' And with a smile she
added: 'But Henri, you did such a good job I might have to
stay a little longer to say more rosaries for the children. And
that will keep me quite busy because you know there are
quite a few.' Then — one day, sitting in her chair behind the
window, with her old prayer book in her hands, she simply
bowed her head and left us. And her face was full of peace
and light."[245]

Later in Nouwen's book about aging from which I have
been quoting, Nouwen writes that:

"Death can be made into our final gift. It is this sense
of hope that we want to strengthen. When aging can
be experienced as a growing by giving, not only of
mind and heart, but of life itself, then it can become a
movement towards the hour when we can say with
the author of the Second Letter to Timothy: *'As for
me, my life is already being poured away as a liba-
tion, and the time has come for me to be gone. I have
fought the good fight to the end. I have run the race to
the finish; I have kept the faith.'*(2 Tim 4:6-7)"[246]

While doing research for my book I came upon a book
called *Mystery of Mary* by a French Thomist theologian,
Marie-Dominique Philippe, O.P. [247] I found in the book
these profound reflections:

"Mary died to teach us how to die in love of Christ...

"Death is becoming hidden in God.

"In the face of death the enigma of human existence
reaches its climax. Man is not only the victim of pain
and the progressive deterioration of his body; he is
also, and more deeply, tormented by the fear of final
extinction. But the instinctive judgement of his heart

is right when he shrinks from, and rejects, the idea of a total collapse and a definitive end of his own person. He carries within him the seed of eternity, which cannot be reduced to matter alone, and so he rebels against death. All efforts of technology, however useful they may be, cannot calm his anxieties; the biological extension of his life-span cannot satisfy the desire inescapably present in his heart for a life beyond this life.

"Imagination is completely helpless when confronted with death. Yet the church, instructed by divine revelation, affirms that man has been created by God for a destiny of happiness beyond the reach of earthly trials. Moreover, the Christian faith teaches that bodily death, to which man would not have been subject if he had not sinned, will be conquered; the almighty and merciful Savior will restore man to the wholeness that he had lost through his own fault. God has called man, and still calls him, to be united in his whole being in perpetual communion with himself in the immortality of the divine life. This victory has been gained for us by the risen Christ, who by his own death has freed man from death.

"Faith, presented with solid arguments, offers every thinking person the answer to his questionings concerning his future destiny. At the same time, it enables him to be one in Christ with his loved ones who have been taken from him by death and gives him hope that they have entered into true life with God.

"Certainly, the Christian is faced with the necessity, and the duty, of fighting against evil through many trials, and of undergoing death. But by entering into the paschal mystery and being made like Christ in death, he will look forward, strong in hope, to the resurrection.

This is true not only of Christians but also of all men of good will in whose heart grace is invisibly at work. Since

Christ died for all men, and the ultimate vocation of man is in fact one, that is, a divine vocation, we must hold that the Holy Spirit offers to all the possibility of being united with this paschal mystery in a way known only to God.

"Such is the great mystery of man, enlightening believers through the Christian revelation. Through Christ and in Christ light is thrown on the enigma of pain and death which overwhelms us without his Gospel to teach us. Christ has risen, destroying death by his own death; he has given us the free gift of life so that as sons in the Son we may cry out in the Spirit, saying: *Abba, Father!*"

I wish to end this chapter of "At the Gates of Eternity" with more reflections from the writings of Charles Rich. After his conversion from a Chasidic Jewish background to the Catholic faith when he was thirty-three, he spent the rest of his years until his ninety-ninth birthday wishing he could die and be united with his beloved Christ. Here are some of his thoughts about eternity:

"The only reason why we have to go through all we do is the fact that, loving us as He does, the purpose for which we have been created shall one day be accomplished, that of being the happy subjects of His kingdom of love, and this forever and ever."[248]

"Death is the entrance into the kingdom of God, for though we may have some perception of what this kingdom is while we are in the body, we cannot fully possess its hidden inner riches until we die. 'What little sense you have!..Did not the Messiah have to undergo all this so as to enter into his glory?'(Luke 24: 25-26). In these words God Himself wishes to point out that there is no entering into His eternal kingdom of love and bliss until by means of the sufferings we have to go through we will have 'paid the last penny' (Matthew 5:26) which our sins have incurred."[249]

"Suffering deprives us of bodily pleasures, and it does so for the purpose of bestowing on the soul a delight to be had in no other way. We cannot know what the delight of God is unless we go through all manner of anguish...Pain is bitter, but what it leads to is infinitely sweet...It is sheer misery to be afflicted in body and soul, but we have the Son of God giving us an example in this regard...We cannot lose when we suffer, we can only gain the graces we receive as the result of that suffering...God allows no evil to exist from which He cannot derive greater glory for His elect souls."[250]

"Suffering detaches us from the accidental things of this life so that thus detached we may get the grace to cling and cleave to what is permanent and essential in it...To dispose ourselves for the grace of detachment, it is not enough to read spiritual books and to meditate on things eternal — we must suffer, and this in both body and mind...To know what God is like we have to suffer, since without suffering we can never have a living experience of all that He Is in his Essential Self."[251]

"We cannot know Christ unless we suffer, since it is by means of the Cross that He can be recognized, felt and believed in. We cannot know what the divine sweetness of God is like unless we ask for the grace to bear whatever we have to in the right Christian way."[252]

"Old Age is nothing in the eyes of God because He sees the eternal youth which will one day be ours. Sickness and disease concern Him not because He knows that what we now call health is itself a kind of sickness; and life, death.

"The devil tries to depress us by separating us from the truths of faith. There is nothing he hates so much as our belief in the life to come."[253]

I love these sublime ideas of my mentor Charles Rich, but if you are looking for some ideas about how a more typical man succeeded in remaining joyful during unpleasant aspects of the concrete process of dying, you might want to look at a charming book by a Catholic hospice worker, Mary Anne McCrickland Benas, called *Dancing with God*

Through the Evening of Life — Reflections from a Dying Man.[254]

Prayer:

So now, dear God, what excuse do we have not to pray continually for the faith, hope and love of those whose words we have read? May the devil never snatch us out of your hands. And when we are overwhelmed by doubt, fear and despair, may we hope against hope in your promises.

FOR PERSONAL REFLECTION AND GROUP SHARING:
1. Of the lines in this section about the gates of eternity, which spoke to you most?
2. Can you tuck in this book pages with favorite sayings you have found about the gates of eternity?

Rites and Prayers

In close relationship to the sick and the dying, I have found the words of the rites and prayers of the Church consoling: full of realism and hope.

You may or may not know that the sacrament of anointing of the sick is no longer administered by the priest only just before death, but at any time when health is seriously threatened.

For the rite of anointing, there is a candle symbolizing the light of Christ and resurrection, and also special oil. There are opening prayers with members of the family and friends participating. It is extremely beneficial, even for those not in mortal sin, to make a general confession. This means confessing in general terms all the sins of ones life, such as "I ask God's forgiveness for all the times I spoke harshly to anyone or harshly about someone to others," etc.

One of the most important ways to come to peace of mind in the later years of life is to be sure you have forgiven everyone who ever hurt you in any way. After all, the words of the prayer Jesus gave us says "Forgive us our trespasses as we forgive those who trespass against us."

In the Rite of Anointing, after confession, more prayers are said, and then the priest using his thumb makes the sign of the cross with the oil on the body of the sick person. Scriptures are read about healing and faith and the priest lays hands on the head of the person who is seriously ill.

The Mass for the Dead wonderfully combines the celebration of the life of the person who has moved on to eternity with prayers for his or her immortal soul and prayers for the grieving family and friends. Here are some of the prayers that can be said:

"Lord, those who die still live in your presence and your saints rejoice in complete happiness. Listen to our prayers for (name of the person) who has passed from the light of this world, and bring him (her) to the joy of eternal radiance."

"By the suffering and death of your Son free him (her) from the bonds of his (her) sins and bring him (her) to endless joy in your presence. We ask this through Christ our Lord. Amen."

In participating in the Liturgy for beloved dead and anticipating ones own death, it seems that all the words of the Mass come alive; for what is the Sacrifice if not the promise that the Body and Blood of Christ shed for us is to free us from our sins and open the gates of heaven to us?

It is the same with the Hail Mary. We pray it over and over again in the rosary, but when we are actually grieving the death of a loved one or readying ourselves for death, then the words "Pray for us sinners, now and at the hour of our death," have a strength far beyond our normal repetition of that prayer. How happy we shall be when our time comes to see our Holy Mother waiting for us with open arms!

The night prayer of the Church, formerly called Compline, is full of comfort for those who find the darkness of the late hours conducive to fear of the future or of death. My husband who had an allergy to most devotional prayers,

had a great love for these more formal prayers that have
been recited for so many centuries.

Here are some words from this beautiful prayer:

"Keep us, we pray, O King of kings,
beneath your own almighty wings.
Forgive us, Lord, through Christ your Son,
Whatever wrong this day we've done;
Your peace give to the world, O Lord,
That man might live in one accord.
Enlighten us, O blessed Light,
And give us rest throughout this night.
O strengthen us, that for your sake,
We all may serve you when we wake."
From Wednesday Night Prayer
Here is a hymn from Sunday Night Prayer:
Abide with me; fast falls the eventide;
The darkness deepens, Lord, with me abide;
When other helpers fail, and comforts flee,
Help of the helpless, O abide with me.
Swift to its close ebbs out life's little day;
Earth's joys grow dim, its glories pass away;
Change and decay in all around I see;
O Thou who changest not, abide with me.
Hold Thou thy Cross before my closing eyes;
Shine through the gloom, and point me to the skies;
Heaven's morning breaks, and earth's vain shadows
flee;
In life, in death, O Lord, abide with me.
Wednesday Night Prayer continues with these verses
from Psalm 31:1-6:
"In you, O Lord, I take refuge....
Be a rock of refuge for me...
Into your hands I commend my spirit.
It is you who will redeem me, Lord."

Later comes a prayer for trust: "May you be our joy at
the turning points of life and our reward at its end."
From Psalm 130:
"Out of the depths I cry to you, O Lord...
If you, O Lord, should mark our guilt,
Lord who would survive?
But with you is found forgiveness:
for this we revere you...
My soul is waiting for the Lord,
I count on his word..."
Based on the Gospel according to Luke (2:29-32) we
have these words:
"Protect us Lord, as we stay awake; watch over us as
we sleep, that awake, we may keep watch with Christ
and asleep, rest in his peace."
After the concluding prayer, "May the all-powerful Lord
grant us a restful night and a peaceful death," comes a hymn in
honor of the Blessed Virgin. My favorite is the Salve Regina:
Hail, Holy Queen, Mother of Mercy
our life, our sweetness, and our hope.
To you do we cry,
poor banished children of Eve.
To you do we send up our sighs
mourning and weeping in this valley of tears.
Turn then, most gracious advocate,
your eyes of mercy towards us,
and after this our exile
show unto us the blessed fruit of your womb, Jesus.
O clement, O loving,
O sweet Virgin Mary.

The above prayers are taken from Wednesday Night
Prayer. There are many other beautiful ones for the other
nights of the week. I highly recommend that all readers of
my book get hold of a little pamphlet of the night prayer of

the Church to read before going to sleep each night. Every Catholic bookstore has these pamphlets.

One of the most beautiful prayers for our lives in general, but especially when fearing death, is that of Ven. John Henry Cardinal Newman.

LEAD KINDLY LIGHT
Poem and Hymn
Lead, kindly Light, amid the encircling gloom,
Lead thou me on;
The night is dark, and I am far from home,
Lead thou me on;
Keep thou my feet; I do not ask to see
The distant scene; one step enough for me.
I was not ever thus, nor prayed that thou
Shouldst lead me on;
I loved to choose and see my path; but now
Lead thou me on.
I loved the garish day, and, spite of fears,
Pride ruled my will: remember not past years.
So long thy power hath blest me, sure it still
Will lead me on
O'er moor and fen, o'er crag and torrent, till
The night is gone,
And with the morn those Angel faces smile,
Which I have loved long since, and lost awhile.

FOR PERSONAL REFLECTION AND GROUP SHARING:

1. You might want to assemble some of your own favorite lines from rites or prayer books and make them into a little booklet you could have near your bed.

2. Some Christians find peace in writing down what they would like written on their tombstones or what kind of funeral they would prefer. If you wish to pursue this, you can give a copy to someone close who would be expected to carry out your wishes.

CONCLUSION

"They shall see the Lord face to face and bear His name on their foreheads. And night shall be no more. They will need no light from lamps or the sun, for the Lord God shall give them light, and they shall reign forever." (The Book of Revelations 22: 4-5)

The work on *Seeking Christ in the Crosses and Joys of Aging* has been quite a journey for me personally. When I started research and writing, I was fearful, discouraged, and even somewhat despairing about my earthly future. Now I find I am full of hope and raring to go! I hope, with the grace of God, your experience in reading my book is equally positive.

I want to conclude with a few recommendations for follow-up. The first one is to read and pray Scripture every day. The Word has a power that no other reading can possibly have since it was inspired by the Holy Spirit in a unique manner to increase our faith, hope and love. Secondly, it is important to spend at least as much time reading the doctors of the Church and lives of the saints or watching Christian TV as might be spent on worldly media. The reason is simple — advertisers sponsor programs, for the most part, that put you in the mood to buy their products, not in the mood for communion with God. Too much time with the world usually drains one of faith.

A powerful foretaste of eternity can be experienced by listening to the great classical music works based on Scripture or the Mass. Many of these works by such composers as Bach, Mozart, Beethoven, Mahler and others directly express a Christian vision of eternity. The beauty of the music in a certain way lifts the veil that separates us from the bliss of heaven.

My twin-sister, Carla De Sola, a sacred dancer, was reading this book. She thought of a way you might not have imagined to open yourself to God even if you are mostly confined to the house or the bed. Here is how she wanted her suggestion conveyed:

"Henri Nouwen, describing his grandmother's last days, when she was 'knitting, knitting, knitting...' as well as praying the rosary, reminded me that there's yet another way of praying, while sitting or lying in bed, where no materials of any kind are needed. The prayer engages only hands and soul and is in the form of sacred dance: the simplest form is *praying for others*. You are lying on your back in bed, hands folded over your chest. Feel the movement of your breath, gently in and out...releasing your hands, extend them outward, up and back to yourself with a feeling of gathering, drawing back to yourself all the prayers and needs of others you can imagine. Your hands are once again resting on your chest, connecting your heart with the prayers. After a minute or so, raise you hands upward, with the intention of *releasing* the prayers to God.

A prayer/gesture to the Hail Mary is another possibility:

Begin with your hands folded over your chest, as above:

Hail Mary, full of grace, the Lord is with you.

Release one hand upward, as if in greeting to Mary.

Blessed are you among women, and blessed is the fruit of your womb, Jesus.

Raising your other hand, fan both outward, and in a continuous motion, circle your hands downward, ending with both hands close to your body, cupped together, palms facing upward.

Holy Mary, Mother of God, pray for us sinners, now and at the hour of death.

Reach with your hands toward your feet (still lying flat). Turning your palms face

downward, slowly draw your hands up over your body, as if receiving Mary's blessing from toe to head. Opening your arms to the side, return your hands to your heart. Open your arms sideways, forming the ancient 'orans' position of praise.

Let us dance through the gates of eternity."

One last thought. A decision that has greatly enhanced my own years since turning sixty involved making a formal consecration of the rest of my life to Christ. This has taken two forms. The first one is becoming what I call a "Woman of Jesus." This involved making a private vow never to marry again so as to belong wholly to Christ. I also chose to live very simply, wearing a blue dress, no make-up or jewelry, to be able to give as much as possible of my funds to the needy. Thinking others might be interested in aspects of this option, whether married or single, I called this way of life "Women and Men of Jesus." There are no dues, no meetings, but there is some correspondence. If you are interested, send me a stamped, self-addressed envelope to P.O. Box 9785 Corpus Christi, TX 78469, and I will send you a flyer about it.

After making my private vow, I felt led by Christ to join an emerging religious community of sisters called Handmaids of Nazareth. This community of women with a traditional spirituality but a contemporary life-style is designed to make it possible both for younger women and older women to participate. Some will live together in Houses of Eucharistic Adoration, but others will live wherever they were before, for example, taking care of the elderly or children or needing to live in a certain town for reasons of work or being too disabled to move around. If you are an unmarried woman (including divorced/annulled) and interested in more information, write to Handmaids of

Nazareth Office F, P.O. Box 507, Pittsford, NY 14534.

Whether you are an elderly woman or man, you should know that there are many late vocation opportunities opening up. Many men are becoming deacons and others priests even in their seventies. Religious orders that restricted entry to younger people have now found ways to include the elderly. There are many opportunities for married and single lay people to join together in Secular Orders or in pious movements to enhance their own spirituality and enjoy greater fellowship.

I am presently a consecrated widow in the community of The Society of Our Lady of the Most Holy Trinity.

ENDNOTES

WHAT DOES AGING FEEL LIKE?

Doing It Your Own Way

[1] Kathryn Etters Lovatt, "The Year Alice Moved to the Attic," I am Becoming the Woman I've Wanted, edited by Sandra Haldeman Martz (Watsonville, CA: Papier-Mache Press, 1994), pp. 209-214.

[2] Ibid., p. 214.

[3] Ronald Blythe, The View in Winter: Reflections on Old Age (NY: Penguin Books, 1980).

[4] Ibid., p. 143.

[5] Sarah Allen, "Clay," I am Becoming..., pp.187-189.

[6] Virginia Woolf, Mrs. Dalloway, (NY: Harcourt, Brace and World, Inc.).

[7] Ibid., p. 75.

[8] Ibid., p.85.

[9] Arnold Bennett, The Old Wives' Tale (NY: Random House, 1908).

[10] Ibid.

[11] George Lawton, Aging Successfully (NY: Columbia University Press, 1946).

[12] Excerpts from Aging Successfully, copyright 1946 Columbia University Press, are reprinted with permission of the publisher.

[13] Ibid., p. 239.

[14] Jayne Relaford Brown, "Finding Her Here" from I am Becoming..., p. 1.

New Sources of Joy

[15] Marilyn Zukerman, "After Sixty," I am Becoming....

[16] Arnold Bennett, The Old Wives' Tale, p. 518.

[17] Glyn Hughes, Bronte (NY: St. Martin's Press, 1996).

[18] Ibid., pp. 322-323.

[19] Constance Bereford-Howe, The Book of Eve (NY: Avon, 1973).

[20] Ibid., p.161.

[21] Ibid., p. 163.

[22] Virginia Woolf, Mrs. Dalloway, pp. 63-64.

[23] Ronald Blythe, The View in Winter, p. 41.

[24] Virginia Woolf, Mrs. Dalloway, pp. 119-120.

[25] Ibid., p. 247.

[26] Bessie and Sadie Delaney, Having Our Say: The Delaney Sisters' First Hundred Years (Kodansha International, 1993) pp. 258-259.

[27] George Lawton, Aging Successfully, p. 2.

Loneliness and Closeness

[28] Mary Sue Koeppel, "In Praise," I am Becoming..., p. 192.

[29] Arnold Bennett, The Old Wives' Tale, p. 494.

[30] Ronald Blythe, The View in Winter, p. 147.

[31] Ibid.

[32] Kay Loftus, "Spring Surge," I am Becoming..., p. 191.

[33] Virginia Woolf, Mrs. Dalloway, p. 45.

[34] "Elbert" (Author regrets losing this reference).

[35] Naomi Halperin Spigle, "A Living Will," I am Becoming..., p. 216.

[36] George Lawton, Aging Successfully, p. 157.

[37] Ronald Blythe, The View in Winter, pp. 58-60.

[38] Ibid., pp. 257-258.

[39] Ibid.

Physical Pain

[40] Ronald Blythe, The View in Winter, pp. 147-149.

[41] Ibid., p. 152.

[42] The Correspondence of Shelby Foote and Walker Percy, edited by Jay Tolson (NY: W.W. Norton and Co., Inc., 1997), p. 233.

[43] Ibid., p. 260.

[44] Ibid., p. 233.

Approaching Death

[45] Virginia Woolf, Mrs. Dalloway, p. 265.

[46] Ronald Blythe, The View in Winter, p. 148.

[47] Ellen Kort, "If Death were a Woman", I am Becoming..., pp. 217-218.

[48] Ibid., p. 207.

[49] Florida Scott-Maxwell, quoted from The Measure of My Days (NY: Alfred Knopf, 1968) p. 138 in Aging, The Fulfillment of Life, by Nouwen, Henri J.M.. and Gaffney, Walter J., (NY: Image Press, 1976) pp.27-28.

[50] Ronald Blythe, The View in Winter, p. 40.

Heroes and Heroines of Aging

[51] Parade Magazine, Arizona Republic, 12/12/93.

[52] Parade Magazine, Arizona Republic, 4/19/98 and 4/26/98.

[53] Tuesdays with Morrie, Brilliance Corporation, Grand Haven, Michigan 49417.

54 Richard Attenborough, The Words of Gandhi (NY: Newmarket Press, 1982).
55 Ibid.
56 Eleanor Roosevelt, On My Own (NY: Harper, 1958).
57 Ibid.
58 Pablo Casals, Joys and Sorrows:Reflections by Pablo Casals as told to Albert E. Kahn (NY: Simon and Schuster, 1970).
59 Otto Kallir, Grandma Moses, the Artist Behind the Myth (NY: C.N. Potter - Crown, 1982).

WISDOM FROM THE PROFESSIONALS

From Literature
60 La Rochefoucauld, quoted in Chicken Soup for the Woman's Soul, edited by Canfield, Hansen, Hawthorne, and Shimoff (Deerfield Beach, FL: Health Communications, Inc., 1996) p. 258.
61 Ronald Blythe, The View in Winter: Reflections on Old Age (NY: Penguin Books, 1980), pp. 15-16.
62 Ibid., p. 15.
63 Ibid.
64 Ibid., p. 21.
65 Ibid., p. 69.
66 Ibid., p. 101.
67 Ibid., p. 185.
68 Ibid., quoted from Charles Lamb, The Superannuated Man, pp. 26-27.

From Medical and Sociological Research
69 "Memory Loss and Aging," Alzheimer's Association of Tasmania, 5/24/97, pp. 1-3.
70 Wise Choices Beyond Mid-life, by Scott, Schrempt, Weiss, and Soldz, quoted in an article "60 and Still Going," in Arizona Republic, October 14, 1977, p. C1-C2.
71 Ronald Blythe, The View in Winter, p. 3.
72 "Going for Old," summarizing data from Successful Aging by John W. Rowe, M.D. and Robert L. Kahn, Ph.D. - Pantheon Books, in Arizona Republic, April 9,1998, p. HL1.
73 American Medical News, Sept. 25, 1995, p. 11.
74 Robert L. Kahn, Ph.D. Successful Aging, quoted in "Going for Old," Arizona Republic, p. HL 1.
75 Sharon Curtin, Nobody Ever Died of Old Age (Boston and Toronto: Little, Brown & Co., 1972) p. 56 quoted in Nouwen, Aging, The Fulfillment of Life (NY: Image Books, 1976).
76 Gail Sheehy, "How to Age Well," in Parade Magazine, Arizona Republic, April 26, 1998, pp. 4-5.

[77] Betty Friedan, The Fountain of Age (Tape).
[78] Ronald Blythe, The View in Winter, p. 5.
[79] Ibid., p. 7.
[80] Ibid., p. 12.
[81] Ibid., pp. 22-23.
[82] Ibid., p. 43.
[83] Ibid., pp. 51-52.
[84] Ibid., p. 71.
[85] Ibid., p. 88.
[86] Ibid., pp. 167-169.
[87] See Ibid., pp. 192-194.
[88] Ibid., p. 238.

From Psychology
[89] Harriet Lerner, Ph.D., quoted by editor Lisa Liebman in "Getting Over Getting Older," Psychology Today, (New York, 12/96), p. 6.
[90] See Ibid., Psychology Today, Susan Scarf Merrell, pp. 34-40.
[91] Ibid.
[92] Dr. Wayne E. Oates, "Getting Older Without Fear," CARE NOTES.
[93] For an account of dealing with this tragedy that could be of use to other survivors of suicide, see the chapter "Out of the Depths I Cry unto Thee," in my autobiography, En Route to Eternity (Highland, NY: Miriam Press, 1994).
[94] George Lawton, Aging Successfully (NY Columbia University Press, 1946).
[95] Ibid., p. ix.
[96] Ibid., pp. 3-5.
[97] Ibid., p. 22.
[98] Ibid., p. 4.
[99] Ibid., p. 41.
[100] Ibid., pp. 9-10.
[101] For more information about groups called Recovery, Inc. (not 12 steps) call their headquarters in Chicago at 312-337-5661.
[102] George Lawton, Aging Successfully, pp. 45-50.
[103] Ibid., p. 57.
[104] Ibid., p. 51.
[105] Ibid., p. 100.
[106] Ibid., p. 141.
[107] Ibid., p. 145.
[108] Ibid., p. 174 ff.
[109] Ibid., p. 190 ff.
[110] Ibid., p. 207.
[111] Nouwen, Henri J.M. and Walter J. Gaffney Aging, The Fulfillment of Life (NY: Image Books, 1976).

112 Ibid., p. 29 ff.
113 Ibid., p. 36.
114 Ibid., p. 39 ff.
115 Ibid., pp. 59-60.
116 Henri J. M. Nouwen, With Burning Hearts: A Meditation on the Eucharistic Life (Maryknoll, NY: Orbis Books, 1994), pp. 53-54.

WISDOM FROM THE CHURCH

From the Inspiration of Christian Spirituality

117 St. John Chrysostom, Office of Readings.
118 St. Augustine, Office of Readings.
119 The Book of Margery Kempe, trans. Tony D. Triggs (Liguori, MO: Triumph Books, 1995).
120 Ibid., see p. 197.
121 St. Ignatius of Loyola, The Spiritual Exercises and Selected Works, edited by George E. Ganss, S.J. (NY: Paulist Press, 1991).
122 Ibid., p. 340.
123 Ronda Chervin, Quotable Saints, p. 101.
124 Ibid.
125 Ibid., p. 100.
126 Ibid., p. 101.
127 Ibid., p. 102.
128 Richard Johnson, Ph.D. "Growing Older Gracefully: The Endless Horizon of God's Love" Liguorian Magazine, January 1992–December 1992.
129 Permission has been granted to reprint parts of "Growing Older Gracefully" by Richard Johnson, Ph.D. originally published in 1992 issues of Liguorian Magazine, One Liguori Drive, Liguori, MO 63057
130 Ibid., Jan, 1992, p. 54.
131 Ibid., p. 55.
132 Ibid., March 1992, see p. 45.
133 Ibid., April 1992, p. 46.
134 Ibid., p. 47.
135 Ibid., June, 1992, p. 45.
136 Ibid., p. 45.
137 Ibid., Aug. 1992, see p. 63.
138 Ibid., Oct. 1992, see p. 21. See also Nov. issue.
139 Ibid., Aug. 1992, p. 53.
140 Ibid., Nov. 1992.
141 Ibid., p. 61.
142 Ibid.
143 Charles Rich, Reflections (Peterhsam, MA: St. Bede's Press, 1977).

[144] Ibid., pp. 31-34.
[145] Ibid., p. 7.
[146] Ibid., p. 29.
[147] Ibid., p. 56.
[148] Ibid., pp. 95-97.
[149] Ibid., p. 39.

From the Witness of the Saints About Aging
[150] Charles Rich, Reflections, p.2.
[151] Ibid., pp. 5-6.
[152] Peter Brown, Augustine of Hippo (Berkeley, CA: University of California Press, 1969) p. 408.
[153] Ibid.
[154] Ibid., p. 414.
[155] Ibid, p. 418.
[156] Ibid., p. 431.
[157] Ibid., p. 43.2
[158] Johannes Jorgensen, St. Francis of Assisi (NY: Image Books, 1955), p. 221 ff.
[159] Ibid., p. 221.
[160] Ibid., p. 222.
[161] Ibid., pp. 222-223.
[162] Ibid., see p. 224.
[163] Ibid., pp. 231-235.
[164] Angela of Foligno, The Complete Works, trans. by Paul Lachance, O.F.M. (Mahwah, NJ: Paulist Press, 1993).
[165] Ibid.
[166] Ibid., p. 16.
[167] Ibid., p. 253.
[168] Ibid., p. 264.
[169] Ibid., p. 281.
[170] Ibid., p. 302.
[171] Ibid., see pp. 308-311 for Angela's last letter.
[172] Ibid., pp. 312-316.
[173] Ibid.
[174] The Collected Works of St. Teresa of Avila, Volume One. Trans. by Kieran Kavanaugh, O.C.D. and Otilio Rodriquez, O.C.D. (Washington, D.C.: ICS Publications, 1976).
[175] Ibid., p. 5.
[176] Ibid, pp. 264-265.
[177] Ibid, p. 265.
[178] Ibid., p. 387.
[179] William Thomas Walsh, St. Teresa of Avila, a Biography (Milwaukee: Bruce Publishing Co., 1943).

180 St. Teresa of Avila, Collected Works, pp. 363-365.
181 Joseph Oppitz, C.SS.R. Autumn Memoirs of St. Alphonsus Liguori (Liguori, MO: Liguori Publications, no date).
182 Ibid., pp. 74-75.
183 Ibid., see p. 75 to end of booklet.
184 Selections for this section come from Elizabeth Seton: Selected Writings, edited by Ellen Kelly and Annabelle Melville (NY: Paulist Press, 1987) See especially p. 354 ff.
185 Ibid.
186 C. Bernard Ruffin, The Life of Brother Andre the Miracle Worker of St. Joseph (Huntington, IN: Our Sunday Visitor, 1988).
187 Ibid., pp. 57-58.
188 Ibid., pp. 65.
189 Ibid., p. 69.
190 Ibid., pp. 122, 129.
191 Ibid., pp. 124, 151.
192 Ibid., p. 126.
193 Ibid., pp. 137-138.
194 Ibid., p. 159.
195 Ibid., pp. 190-194.
196 Guy Gaucher, Histoire d'une vie: Therese Martin (Paris: Les Editions du Cerf, 1996) and Stephane-Joseph Piat, O.F.M., Celine, Sister Genevieve of the Holy Face, trans. by the Carmelite Sisters of the Eucharist (San Francisco, CA: Ignatius, 1997).
197 Piat, pp. 34-58.
198 Ibid., p. 38.
199 Gaucher, pp. 109-110.
200 Piat, p. 38.
201 Ibid., p. 40.
202 Ibid., p. 47.
203 Ibid., p. 58.
204 Ibid., p. 139.
205 Ibid., p. 135.
206 Ibid., p. 147.
207 Ibid., p. 149.
208 Ibid., p. 150.
209 Ibid., p. 151.
210 Ibid., p. 171.
211 Ibid., p. 177.
212 Mother Teresa, Jesus the Word to be Spoken - compiled by Brother Angelo Devananda Scolozzi, (Ann Arbor, MI: Servant Books, 1986); Sister Sue Mosteller, My Brother My Sister, (NY: Paulist Press, 1972); Roger Royle, Mother Teresa, A Life in Pictures (San Francisco: Harper, 1992).

[213] Mother Teresa, Jesus the Word to be Spoken, p. xii.
[214] Ibid., p. 14.
[215] Ibid., p. 31.
[216] Ibid., p. 36.
[217] Ibid., p. 39.
[218] Ibid., Mosteller, My Brother My Sister, p. 65.
[219] Roger Royle, Mother Teresa, A Life in Pictures, p. 41.
[220] Ibid., p. 43.

At the Gates of Eternity

[221] Dietrich Von Hildebrand, Jaws of Death:Gates of Heaven (Manchester, NH: Sophia Institute Press, 1991).
[222] Ronda Chervin, Victory Over Death (Petersham, MA: St. Bede's Publications, 1985).
[223] Catechism of the Catholic Church (Rome: Libreria Editrice Vaticana, 1994).
[224] St. Augustine – Tract on the First Letter of John (Tract. 4: PL 35, 2008-2009) – Office of Readings, Friday, 6th Week of Ordinary Time – Book III - p. 218.
[225] Aquinas, St. Thomas, Summa Theologica (Chicago: Great Books of the Western World, Volumes 19 and 20, Encyclopedia Brittanica, 1952) You can find long sections about the immortality of the soul and the eternal destiny of the soul in these Volumes. Specific references include these: Volume 19: Questions 75-102, p. 609ff.; Volume 20: Questions 1-99, pp. 885-997.
[226] This quotation comes from an article by Fr. Charles M. Mangan, a priest of the Diocese of Sioux Falls, SD, "The Glorified Body, The Promise of Christ's Resurrection," from a Franciscan University of Steubenville magazine, pp. 30-31, concerning the teaching on the resurrected body by Thomas Aquinas from the Summa Theologica, Question 85, article 1.
[227] Peter Kreeft, Everything You Ever Wanted to Know about Heaven (Ignatius Press, 1990).
[228] Ronda Chervin, Quotable Saints (Ann Arbor, MI: Servant Publications, 1992), p. 45ff.
[229] The Letters of St. Bernard of Clairvaux, trans. by Bruno Scott James (Kalamazoo, MI: Cisterican Publications, 1998).
[230] Ibid., p. 481.
[231] Ibid., p. 484.
[232] Ibid., p. 517.
[233] Ibid., p. 169
[234] Ibid., p. 521.
[235] Ronda Chervin, Quotable Saints, p. 45 ff.

236   Ronald Blythe, The View in Winter, p. 258.
237   Ibid., p. 238.
238   Ibid.
239   Ibid., p. 242.
240   Ibid., p. 256.
241   Ibid., p. 263.
242   Ibid., pp. 265-267.
243   Ibid., p. 233.
244   Fr. Luke Zimmer, SS.CC., A Journey Through Life: CHOSEN (Santa Barbara, CA: Queenship Publishing Company, 1997).
245   Nouwen, Gaffney, pp. 61-62.
246   Ibid., p. 14.
247   Fr. Marie-Dominique Philippe, O.P., Mystery of Mary, trans. by Andre Faure-Beaulieu (Paris: La Colombe, 1958).
248   Charles Rich, Reflections, p. 10.
249   Ibid., p. 11.
250   Ibid., pp. 23-24.
251   Ibid., pp. 58-59.
252   Ibid., p. 61.
253   Ibid., 87.
254   Mary Anne McCrickland Benas, Dancing with God through the Evening of Life (Oak Lawn, IL: CMJ Marian Publications, 1998).

BIBLIOGRAPHY

Alzheimer's Association of Tasmania, Memory Loss and Aging, 5/24/97

Angela of Foligno, The Complete Works, trans. by Paul LaChance, O.F.M. (Mahwah, NJ: Paulist Press, 1993)

Aquinas, St. Thomas, Summa Theologica (Chicago: Great Books of the Western World, Volumes 19 and 20, Encyclopedia Brittanica, 1952)

Attenborough, Richard, The Words of Gandhi (NY: Newmarket Press, 1982)

Augustine, St., Tract on the First Letter of John (Tract. 4: PL 35, 2008-2009) – Office of Readings, Friday, Sixth Week in Ordinary Time, Book III - p. 218

Avanti Greeting Cards, COLORS, Detroit, MI, 1991

Beauvoir, Simone de, The Coming of Age (NY: C.P. Putnam's Sons, 1972)

Benas, Mary Anne McCrickland, Dancing with God through the Evening of Life: Reflections from a Dying Man (Oak Lawn, IL: CMJ Marian Publications, 1998)

Bennet, Arnold, The Old Wives' Tale (NY: The Modern Library Random House, 1908)

Beresford-Howe, Constance, The Book of Eve (NY: Avon Books, 1973)

Blythe, Ronald, The View in Winter: Reflections on Old Age (NY: Penguin Books, 1980)

Brown, Peter, Augustine of Hippo (Berkeley, CA: University of California Press, 1969)

Canfield, Hansen, Hawthorne, and Shimoff, eds. Chicken Soup for the Woman's Soul, (Deerfield Beach, FL: Health Communications, Inc., 1996)

Casals, Pablo, Joys and Sorrows: Reflections by Pablo Casals as told to Albert E. Kahn (NY: Simon and Schuster, 1970)

Catechism of the Catholic Church (Rome: Libreria Editrice Vaticano, 1994) English translations available in any bookstore.

Chervin, Ronda, Victory Over Death (Petersham, MA: St. Bede's Publications, 1985)

Chervin, Ronda De Sola, Quotable Saints (Ann Arbor, MI, Servant, 1992)

The Correspondence of Shelby Foote and Walker Percy, edited by Jay Tolson (NY: W.W. Norton and Co., Inc., 1997)

Curtin, Sharon R., Nobody Ever Died of Old Age (Boston & Toronto: Little, Brown and Co., 1972)

Delaney, Bessie and Sadie, Having Our Say: The Delaney Sisters' First 100 Years (Kodansha International, 1993)

Friedan, Betty, Fountain of Age, (Tape)

Gaucher, Guy, Histoire d'une vie Therese Martin (Paris: Les Editions du Cerf, 1996)

Hughes, Glyn, Bronte (NY: St. Martin's Press, 1996)

Huxley, Laura, This Timeless Moment (NY: Farrar, Straus & Giroux, 1968)

Ignatius of Loyola: The Spiritual Exercises and Selected Works, Ganss, George, S.J., ed. (NY: Paulist Press, 1991)

Johnson, Richard, Ph.D. "Growing Older Gracefully: The Endless Horizon of God's Love" in Liguorian Magazine, January 1992-December, 1992.

Jorgensen, Johannes, St. Francis of Assisi (NY: Image Books, 1995)

Kallir, Otto, Grandma Moses, The Artist Behind the Myth (NY: C.N. Potter – Crown, 1982)

Kempe, Margery, The Book of Margery Kempe, trans. Tony D. Triggs (Liguori, MO: Triumph Books, 1995)

Kreeft, Peter, Everything You Ever Wanted to Know About Heaven (San Francisco, CA: Ignatius Press, 1990)

Lawton, George, Aging Successfully (NY: Columbia University Press, 1946)

The Letters of St. Bernard of Clairvaux, trans. by Bruno Scott James (Kalamazoo, MI: Cistercian Publications, 1998)

Mangan, Father Charles M., The Glorified Body, the Promise of Christ's Resurrection, (Franciscan University of Steubenville Alumni Magazine, 1997)

Martz, Sandra Haldeman, ed. I am Becoming the Woman I've Wanted (Watsonville, CA: Papier-Mache Press, 1994)

Merrell, Susan Scarf. "Getting Over Getting Older", Psychology Today, Dec. 1996: 34-4

Mother Teresa, Jesus the Word Spoken, compiled by Brother Angelo Devananda Scolozzi (Ann Arbor, MI: Servant Books, 1986)

Neugarten, Bernice, "Grow Old Along With Me! The Best Is Yet To Be", Psychology Today, December 1971, pp. 45-48, 79-81

Nouwen, Henri J.M., With Burning Hearts: A Meditation on the Eucharistic Life (Maryknoll, NY: Orbis Books, 1994)

Nouwen, Henri J.M. and Gaffney, Walter J., Aging, The Fulfillment of Life (NY: Image Press, 1976)

Oates, Dr. Wayne E., Growing Older Without Fear, Care Notes, Abbey Press, St. Meinrad, IN 47577, 1989

The Office of Readings, is a collection of short writings from the Fathers of the Church and saints commenting on the liturgical scripture readings of each day of the Church calendar. It can be found in several forms. In this book there are references both to the one volume edition and to the four-volume edition. The book used by priests, brothers, sisters and lay people through the world for daily meditation can be found in any Catholic bookstore.

Parade Magazine, Cover Story, NYC, NY, 12/12/93

Philippe, Marie-Dominique, O.P. Mystery of Mary, trans. Andre Faure-Beaulieu (Paris: La Colombe, 1958)

Piat, Stephane-Joseph, O.F.M. Celine, Sister Genevieve of the Holy Face, trans. by the Carmelite Sisters of the Eucharist of Colchester, CT (San Francisco, CA: Ignatius Press, 1997 - original 1964 in French)

Potok, Chaim, My Name is Asher Lev (NY: Alfred A Knopf, 1972)

Rich, Charles, Reflections (Petersham, MA: St. Bede 1977)

Roosevelt, Eleanor, On My Own (NY: Harper, 1958)

Rowe, John W., M.D. and Kahn, Robert L., Ph.D. from Successful Aging (Pantheon Books), "Going for Old," in Arizona Republic, April 9, 1998, p. HL 1.

Ruffin, C. Bernard, "Padre Pio: The True Story" (Huntington, IN: Our Sunday Visitor, 1982)

Ruffin, C. Bernard, The Life of Brother Andre - The Miracle Worker of St. Joseph (Huntington, IN: Our Sunday Visitor, 1988)

Scott-Maxwell, Florida, The Measure of My Days (NY: Alfred A. Knopf, 1968) p. 138

Scott, Schrempt, Weiss, and Soldz, Wise Choices After Mid-Life, quoted in an article, "60 and Still Going," in The Arizona Republic, October 14, 1977, p. C1-C2.

Secton, Connie Cone, "60 and Still Going". The Arizona Republic, October 14, 1997. Section C:1-2

Seton, Elizabeth Ann, Elizabeth Seton: Selected Writings, ed. by Ellen Kelly and Annabelle Melville (NY: Paulist Press, 1987)

Von Hildebrand, Dietrich, Jaws of Death: Gates of Heaven (Manchester, NH: Sophia Institute Press, 1991)

Woolf, Virginia, Mrs. Dalloway (NY: Harcourt, Brace and World, Inc., no date – title page ripped out.)

Zimmer, Father Luke, SS.CC., A Journey Through Life: CHOSEN (Santa Barbara, CA: Queenship Publishing Company, 1997)

To order addtional copies of this book:

Please complete the form below and send for each copy

CMJ Marian Publishing
P.O. Box 661 • Oak Lawn, IL 60454
toll free 888-636-6799
call 708-636-2995 or fax 708-636-2855
email jwby@aol.com
www.cmjbooks.com

Name _____

Address _____

City _____ State _____ Zip _____

Phone (_____) _____

	QUANTITY			SUBTOTAL
Crosses and Joys of Aging				
$ 12.95 each	x	_____	=	$ _____
Though I Walk Through the Valley				
$ 14.95 each	x	_____	=	$ _____
The Grunt Padre (hardcover)				
$ 22.95 each	x	_____	=	$ _____
The Grunt Padre (softcover)				
$ 15.95 each	x	_____	=	$ _____
Radiating Christ				
$ 11.00 each	x	_____	=	$ _____
Becoming the Handmaid of the Lord				
$ 13.95 each	x	_____	=	$ _____
The Lost Years				
$ 11.95 each	x	_____	=	$ _____
Healing Meditations of the Gospel of St. John				
$ 9.95 each	x	_____	=	$ _____
Our Lady of the Outfield				
$ 10.95 each	x	_____	=	$ _____
Feminine, Free and Faithful				
$ 9.95 each	x	_____	=	$ _____
Becoming a Woman of God. (With Eileen Spotts)				
$ 9.95 each	x	_____	=	$ _____
+ tax (for Illinois residents only)			=	$ _____
+ 15% for S & H			=	$ _____
TOTAL			=	$ _____

Check # _____ Visa MasterCard Exp Date ___ / ___ / ___

Card # _____

Signature _____